THE TOUCH OF ROY AND DALE

The Impact and Influence of
Roy Rogers, the King of the Cowboys
And Dale Evans, the Queen of the West
As Only Their Fans Could Tell It

Tricia Spencer

"Is She Thinking Of Me or Tom Mix" cover painting by artist Gina Faulk, used with permission from Gina Faulk and the Rogers Family.

Book design and layout by Tricia Spencer and Delaney-Designs.com

Cover design by Tricia Spencer, Dan Bell and Delaney-Designs.com

Custom illustrations by Kimberly Bell

Printed in the United States of America

First Edition - November 2011

ISBN: 978-0-615-49832-4

Acknowledgements

I want to thank all the letter-writing fans, and in some instances, their heirs, and those who wrote essays specifically for this book, for agreeing to share your thoughts and memories with the world. Getting to know you has been a gift.

A huge, heartfelt thank-you must also go to:

My family who graciously accepted my absence from normal life as I spent the last year working around the clock on this book and two others. You mean the world to me, especially my husband who pitched in to help with the nuts-and-bolts work of this book—willingly!

The Rogers Family—Cheryl, Linda Lou, Dusty, Mimi and Dodie—I'm honored that you opened your hearts to this project and participated with such generosity.

Artist Gina Faulk for your kindness in sharing the gorgeous painting that appears on the cover. And Kimberly Bell for your inspired custom illustrations.

Bobbi Jean Bell of OutWest Boutique and Cultural Center, you went above and beyond for a stranger, and I, too, embrace the "serendipity" of our meeting.

Maxine and the other kind folks at Gene Autry Entertainment for so generously spreading the word and sharing the bond of friendship enjoyed by Gene and Roy.

Elton John and Bernie Taupin, your "western spirit" lives in your "Roy Rogers" song, and I so appreciate that you allowed me to share those lyrics with all Roy's fans.

Cathy Guisewite, what can I say? How amazing to have "Cathy" drop by!

The families of Walt LaRue, Governor Lawton Chiles, and Larry James for your kind and dedicated assistance.

Dick Jones, Dean Smith, Donna Martell, and Frank Fiore, how lucky we are that you allowed us to glimpse life with Roy and Dale through your "cowboy" eyes.

Authors Holly George-Warren, Julie Ann Ream, Jamie Nudie, Tomaline "Tommie" Sharpe Lenox, Bobby Copeland, Janet McBride, Jerry Akridge and Raymond E. White, for so eloquently weaving your personal experiences into this book's tapestry.

Texas Children's Hospital for the amazing photo, and Behnke Fine Portraiture of Mokena, Illinois and Blunck's Studios, Inc. of Clinton, Oklahoma for kindly permitting, respectively, the use of the Mackay and Diffendaffer photos.

Damon Wimbley of the Fat Boys, Elsa Ludewig Verderber of the Verdehr Trio, and Tumbleweed Rob Wolfskill of the Tumbling Tumbleweeds, for demonstrating with your talent and musical diversity that Roy and Dale's influence knew no bounds.

Joel "Dutch" Dortch and the Happy Trails Children's Foundation, thank you for all that you do for a cause so dear to Roy and Dale's hearts and for allowing this book to help in that effort.

And, to Billy Graham, for generously and kindly honoring Roy and Dale with your thoughtful reflection.

Finally, for seeing the merit in this project and for spearheading the donation portion of the book sales to the *Happy Trails Children's Foundation*, I owe my greatest thanks to Dan Bell and West Quest, whose commitment to preserving the spirit of the American West helps to keep the Cowboy Culture alive for each new generation.

FOREWORD

My first job was working in the Roy Rogers fan mail office when I was 12 years old. Dad had only been married to Mom for a little over four years, and he was still getting plenty of letters from little girls telling him how upset they were that he had remarried before they had a chance to grow up and marry him (our mother, Arline, had died shortly after my little brother was born.) There were letters from little boys telling him to leave the mushy parts out of his movies when he had only kissed his leading lady on the cheek, and there were letters from little boys and girls from all over the world who wanted to be adopted by Roy and live on his ranch.

Decades later, when Dad was in the hospital, men and women who had been little boys and girls in the 40s, 50s and 60s, wrote to him about how my Dad, their screen hero Roy Rogers, had helped them survive horrible childhoods and grow into strong, productive adults.

Their letters told of how Dad had taken the place of the father they had lost during WWII, Korea or Vietnam, or the father they had lost through divorce or addiction. They said that Dad was the male figure that had stood for right and justice, and he was the reason they had become policemen, firemen, teachers and preachers. He was the good guy in the white hat that showed even the bad guys kindness if warranted.

There were also the letters to Mom, telling her how *Angel Unaware* had changed their lives or those of their friends and loved ones, and how that little book had helped them get through the darkest time of their lives. There were those who wrote telling her that they had chosen careers in the workplace because of the strong yet feminine women she portrayed on the screen. There were also the letters that told of how her show, *A Date With Dale*, was a comfort and source of strength, and how they enjoyed listening to her positive Christian testimony.

Today, as I travel around the country attending Western and film festival events, I am always amazed by how many people come up to me, eager to share their Roy and Dale stories, wanting to relate how Mom and Dad touched their lives.

I am so glad that Tricia is able to share some of their letters with you and that you will now be able to read what my parents have meant to their many friends and fans throughout their lives. Through these letters and the people who wrote them, my parents' lives and careers, their goodness and their caring, will live on.

Cheryl Rogers-Barnett

Roy and Dale's daughter, Cheryl Rogers-Barnett, in the Rose Parade
- photo provided by Robert Kane

THE TOUCH OF ROY AND DALE

Tricia Spencer

The Rogers Family

left to right: Marion (Mimi), Roy "Dusty" Jr., Sandy, Dodie, Dale, Debbie, Linda
Lou, Cheryl, Roy
- photo provided by the Rogers Family

INTRODUCTION

When Leonard Slye was born in Ohio on November 5, 1911, the world couldn't have known that he would one day grow up to become Roy Rogers, the undisputed silver-screen King of the Cowboys. Had the world been privy to the future, celebrations would have rocked the planet the moment that baby boy let loose his first melodic newborn wail.

Little Leonard was still sporting diapers when the first Halloween of his life rolled around. He was too young to think about trick-or-treating, and he was definitely too young to imagine that just a few states to the south, in Texas, his future bride was making her entrance into the world. Frances Octavia Smith, born on October 31, 1912, would one day pursue a career as Frances Fox, then Marian Lee, before embracing her destiny as singing and acting legend, Dale Evans, the Queen of the West.

It would be thirty-two years after that momentous Halloween birth before Roy and Dale would release their first movie together. The 1944 film, "*The Cowboy and the Senorita,*" took both stars to new career heights, and magic happened. The onscreen chemistry of the two talents sparked like a lightning bolt, spawning one of the most successful, long-lived pairings ever on film. The chemistry was onscreen only, for at the time, Roy was married to wife, Arline. Sadly, tragedy struck less than two years later, and Roy lost Arline just a week after the 1946 birth of their son, Roy "Dusty" Rogers, Jr. Alone and grieving, with three small children under his wing to love and protect, Roy had to pick himself by his bootstraps to face life without Arline.

When 1948 was just over the horizon, Roy and Dale made it official, becoming husband and wife on New Year's Eve, 1947. Both had been previously married, and the blending of family became their bedrock. Though Roy and Dale had only one biological child together, they welcomed several adopted children into the fold. Their lives seemed kissed by angels, but in truth, heartache visited often. Roy and Dale lost three of their children far too early. The loss of a child has been known to fracture families, and three separate and tragic losses would be far too much for many parents to bear, but

3

Roy and Dale's belief in God and each other kept their hearts open and their will strong.

It was this undercurrent of profound humanity that turned Roy and Dale's celebrity into something extraordinary. No one could look away from two people who so loved life, each other, their family, their God and their fans. Their dedication to brightening the lives of others, including strangers from all walks of life, all cultures and all beliefs, was more than legendary. It was real. Roy and Dale touched lives.

This book is the story of those lives. While Roy and Dale are the catalyst, the stories that follow are about the people who embraced Roy and Dale for far more than their amazing talents. That Roy was unparalleled as a horseman and a yodeler, or that Dale could write books as eloquently as she could perform, was not the driving force behind the changes they brought to the lives of those who adored them. Fans admired and respected Roy and Dale as celebrities, but even more so as human beings. Because of that straight-to-the-heart connection, people from all over the world allowed Roy and Dale to show them a better way—the "cowboy" way—the spiritual way. It was an awakening.

The excerpts that follow have been culled from nearly 40,000 letters sent to Roy or Dale, or to them as a couple. Most of the letters arrived in the 1990s when health challenges began to plague both Mr. and Mrs. Rogers. It was a time that grown-up boys and long-ago-matured girls who were so deeply influenced by their heroes rallied to support them. They poured out their hearts as enthusiastically as Roy and Dale had supported their fans throughout their lives.

Other letters were sent to Dale after Roy's passing as fans braved their own struggle with the loss of the King of the Cowboys.

That all of these letters were among Roy and Dale's final possessions is a testament to just how much they cared. Boxes and boxes of letters were stuffed with personal stories, photographs, songs, art, poetry and more. And Roy and Dale kept it all.

Some of the excerpts will make you laugh. Others will bring tears. The emotion is sometimes raw and heart wrenching, but as you read the words, the love is evident. There's no need to read between the lines. Fans effused honest emotion with every stroke of their pens.

You will also read essays written by friends and fans whose personal journeys reflect the life and times of Roy and Dale's celebrated heyday and their influence a half a century after it.

Logistically, this book was difficult to produce. After winnowing the letters from multiple thousands down to just two thousand, I attempted to contact everyone from the smaller group. Two thousand letters went out, but the march of time meant that my effort to reach a particular letter-writing fan was frequently defeated. Still, many permissions did arrive, and when they did, even more thoughts and stories spilled forth. It was an amazing journey.

When you read an excerpt attributed to only "a fan," it is because that person granted permission for use of the letter's content but not his or her name. Others asked that only initials or a location be used. Sadly, some stories, so sensitively and beautifully told, simply could not be shared because they were too personal to use without express permission.

The hardest part was whittling this book down to size. With the staggering number of letters, choosing which ones to include was beyond difficult. Those that didn't make it into the book may someday find their way into a future volume. It took years to read all the letters and construct this book, but the effort was an absolute labor of love.

With the contributors' knowledge, I have taken enough literary license to add or subtract words to make an excerpt easier to read. I've also encapsulated some excerpts, allowing me to include even more entries in the book. When new thoughts and stories arrived with permissions, I blended the new with the old. The exception occurred when original words were spoken directly to Roy but current words were remembrances after his death, or related specifically for this book. In those instances, excerpts are split into **"THEN"** and **"NOW."**

But no matter what minor adjustments were made, the changes were never enough to alter the tone or message of the original writer. I employed painstaking effort to preserve the integrity of the letter, for to do anything less would be a disservice to Roy, Dale and the legions of fans who shared their personal stories. Whether the excerpt is only a few words, or multiple pages, it is genuine. Everyone who wrote letters and essays wrote more than what you will read here, but to keep this book from becoming the size of a Los Angeles telephone book, all entries were edited for space. Roy and Dale's history has been told many times, but this book is not a biography. It is a celebration of Roy and Dale's undeniable connection with those who loved them. Except for this introduction, all the words that follow belong to Roy and Dale's friends, family and fans.

Hero is a funny word. It's often bandied about without much regard to where it may land, but true heroes are those who step outside their job and outside themselves without a concern for what rewards or dangers may or may not result from their actions. The word "hero" was made for Roy and Dale.

Sure, both were film heroes, taking down the bad guys with compassion-wrapped gusto. But it was the "outside themselves" real-life giving that made them true heroes. No matter how celebrated Roy and Dale were as singers and actors, no matter how much the Hollywood establishment, or the venues where they performed, tried to poke and prod them to do or say whatever would best sell a film or a product, they stuck to their guns and did as they believed. They made a difference because they *were* different. They were celebrities with the kind of "old shoe" hearts and souls that made them accessible to everyone. And they cared. Plain and simple, they cared.

I never had the pleasure, as many fans you will meet in these pages had, to meet Roy or Dale in their lifetime. But I consider myself very fortunate to have been able to attend both the estate sale held at Roy and Dale's home and the one at their museum. I remember being struck by an overwhelming sense of welcome as I walked into their rambling ranch house. I felt a tear on my cheek as I stood there, for I felt the loss of Roy and Dale wash over me even as I felt their joyful presence.

Celebrity homes sometimes look like show palaces, beautiful but without warmth, but not Roy and Dale's home. It was just that—a home. Inexpensive knick-knacks and eclectic furniture mingled happily with priceless treasures. It was apparent that possessions in the Rogers home had to mean something, something beyond monetary value. Gifts from fans dotted nooks and crannies, and the kitchen was clearly the heartbeat of the house, as kitchens are for families all over the world. I remember thinking that the master bath was about the only place I thought "celebrity." There was a lot of room in there!

Dusty, (Roy Rogers, Jr.,) was present, and he was as approachable as a friend you've known forever. He patiently answered questions and listened as fans went on and on about his famous parents. I can't imagine what it must have been like for him and his siblings to see their parents' home filled to the rafters with strangers who called his parents by their first names as if they'd been on Roy or Dale's speed dial all their lives. But that's how Roy Rogers and Dale Evans made everyone feel—like family.

So turn the pages and meet those who named their children after Roy and Dale or those who changed their lives, careers or faith because of them. Revel in the joy of a modern-day child just discovering that Roy Rogers and Dale Evans magic, or feel the anguish of the troubled ones from long ago who dreamed of Roy as their father or Dale as their mother. Chuckle at the inside stories no one has ever heard, and let your heart fill with the undeniable love that permeates every letter. And most of all, if you're of that age, remember. Allow yourself to walk down your own personal Roy and Dale memory lane as you entertain yourself with the walks of others.

In the pages that follow, you'll see never-before-published photographs of Roy and Dale and the fans who loved them. You'll read original poetry and song lyrics and see original art. You will also see photographs of some of the items I obtained from the Rogers' estate. A numbered horseshoe beside a photograph denotes something actually owned by Roy and Dale, and those horseshoe-designated items are identified at the back of the book.

The photos represent a small sampling of the items I obtained, most of which have long since been transferred to other fans. But in my home, Roy and Dale are ever present. From Roy's brown leather footstool and Dale's basket of silk poinsettias, to occasional tables, wall art, pots and pans, and even the lap desk I used to work on this book while traveling, I see and touch mementos of their life with joyful remembrance on any given day. They are a part of my everyday world—physically through the tangible pieces of their lives that are with me, and soulfully through their extraordinary legacy, and I'm grateful.

Roy and Dale spent all their lives trying to better the lives of others, especially children. The nonprofit Happy Trails Children's Foundation is a living example. Though Roy and Dale are no longer with us, the foundation continues, maintaining a home for at-risk, abused or neglected children in the beautiful high desert area of southern California that Roy and Dale so loved. I am honored that a percentage of the gross proceeds from the sale of this book will go directly to the foundation and play a part in keeping Roy and Dale's dream alive—the dream of a safe and loving world for our nation's greatest treasure, its children.

As someone who grew up with Roy Rogers and Dale Evans leading the way, I feel privileged and blessed to be able to play a small role in honoring the King of the Cowboys, the Queen of the West, and the fans who loved them.

I hope you find much to enjoy in the pages that follow.

Author Tricia Spencer, age 7, with big sister, Donna, age 16

DEAR ROY AND DALE / MOM AND DAD

I've never written a fan letter to anyone. How appropriate my first would be to you. I will always be grateful that you brought me to America and allowed me to become a part of the family, living a life that is beyond what I could have wished for, dreamed of, or prayed for. We had such crazy and wonderful times, as well as some heartbreaking times, in our lives together. I'm equally grateful that you instilled in me the fact that "family" was special and that praying for our families was one of the most important things a person can do in this life.

Dear ones, you were and always will be my heroes. I miss your wit and wisdom.

Love, Mimi
Marion "Mimi" Swift

Roy and Dale's daughter, Mimi Swift
- photo provided by Mimi Swift

9

TRIBUTE

I am pleased to honor two people who have honored us by participating in our crusades and activities beginning way back in 1952. The first time Roy Rogers and Dale Evans were with us in any crusade was in Houston at Rice Stadium, later coming to England for our evangelistic meetings there. They spoke to a children's meeting at the dog track next door to Harringay Arena; an estimated 10,000 adults showed up with 40,000 boys and girls. Roy Rogers rode his cowboy horse, Trigger, around the track, showing off his tricks. But when he and Dale Spoke, it was a simple and straightforward witness to their faith in Christ. Of course, their appearances always created a lot of excitement among the children. I was fortunate to preach to the people who came to see and hear them.

Billy Graham – 2011

**Billy and Ruth Graham with Roy Rogers and Dale Evans in Los Angeles, CA
in 1983**
Photo courtesy of Billy Graham Evangelistic Association.

MEMORIES

There are so many memories. Being the youngest (I so enjoy saying that,) I was exposed to changing times, as were my parents right along with me. I did not make life easy for them, but beyond Roy and Dale being my mom and dad and always being there for me, I admired them because they lived what

they spoke and what they inspired others to do. After Mom's stroke, I especially saw that. She told me she had a weak moment in the hospital and was angry and cried, but then she said, "Buck up, Dale, there's still a lot to be done." Mom did that sometimes—talking out loud to herself, like "Dale, you poot head!" if she thought she goofed something up. So she wasn't about to let a wheelchair keep her from moving ever forward, traveling, giving talks and continuing her concern for others.

Roy and Dale's daughter,
Dodie Patterson
- photo provided by Dodie Patterson

Dusty shows clips in his stage show of Mom and Dad on tour around the country and at state fairs, and no matter how many times I see those clips, tears come to my eyes. Seeing Mom and Dad visiting the hospitals where the joy is alive on the children's faces, or seeing the stands at the fairgrounds filled with children sitting in seats reserved just for them because they couldn't afford tickets, or because they were physically challenged and needed special arrangements, inspires me.

I recall another youthful inspiration—the first time I met Billy Graham at our home in Chatsworth. I was maybe 7 years old or so. I knew of him, but my head was always in the clouds, and I was mainly interested in running around with the dogs. So when I saw him filling the doorway of our living room with that big smile, he caught my attention. But when he shook my hand, I honestly felt a current, and later, when I was 13 and at one of his crusades, I went forward to become a Christian. He always moved me.

Mom and Dad spread goodwill, but they were not alone. Many wrote to them, and I believe that when we all share our positive goodwill with others, and let others know our heart, no one needs to be alone in this world. The positive thoughts cover us. Mom was a firm believer in that philosophy, and she would use the Bible to avoid thinking negative thoughts, quoting Job: "...the thing I most feared has come upon me."

Yes, I was sad at times when Mom and Dad left to do their work and I couldn't go, but there were so many children and families with a feeling of hopelessness, and Mom and Dad gave them hope and a renewed spirit. How could I complain? As an adult, I realized the importance of their work with respect and thankfulness. And I'm grateful, now, that I got to share my parents with the world.

Dodie (Rogers) Patterson

to – Roy

I appreciate very much you autographing the picture of you and Randy Travis that I sent to you. I did not expect to get it back so soon. My son asked me once a few years back what a "Hero" was. I said, "Do you remember how you felt when the men landed on the moon? You felt good inside and you were proud to be an American because of what they had accomplished and what their image stood for. That's the makings of a hero." I told him that in my time of growing up, Roy Rogers was that hero. The image you have projected over the years is one of showing right from wrong, a caring person toward your fellow man, helping others, and especially being a family man. Your life has not only touched those close to you but fans like myself all over the world. You've had quite an impact on a lot of people. I'm just one of many who would like to say thanks for the many memories. Your characteristics that make you the fine person you are have only grown more graceful over the years.

O.D. Spivey, Shelbyville, TN - 12/12/90

to – Roy

The many times I cried because I loved you – like unreal! Thank you for so many wonderful years of YOU!!

Josie Lenard, Grand Junction, CO - 10/4/96

Glen Tymiak with his Roy Rogers Jacket
- photo provided by Glen Tymiak

to – Roy

I am writing to wish you well and to send you a photo of myself and my little Roy Rogers and Trigger jacket that I still have. My parents bought the jacket for me 50 years ago. I've treasured it over all of these years, and I wanted to share this with you.

Glen Tymiak, Yorkton, Saskatchewan, Canada
10/8/96

---

to – Roy

Oh, to remember the Saturday popcorn that smelled up the theater and how all the kids would scream when you were in danger. Your horse, Trigger, was the horse we all wished we had. Roy, you were our hero, our big brother, a person well known and loved by all. A big kiss to you and your beautiful wife, Dale. I thank you!

Darlene Strama, Oak Lawn, IL - 10/18/90

---

to – Dale

Thank you for reviewing the songs and tape that I sent you this past fall and for your kind comments. The fact that you, in your very busy life, took the time to personally answer me thrilled me to no end! But then, you just confirmed what I already knew – you are kind, you are sincere.

Gail Welter, Bay City, MI - 12/12/90

to – Roy

Some thirty odd years ago at a rodeo in Madison Square Garden, New York City, you turned our then little girl's life around. She's now a mother of two in Norwell, Mass, and remembers vividly that very special occasion. She had warts all over the little hands and had suffered much teasing in nursery school and kindergarten. When you were riding your horse around the arena to greet the children, she reached out to shake your hand. You stopped, looked at her hands, took both in yours, and said, "Don't worry about these silly warts, they will all disappear in time!" Sure enough, they did. But before they did, she went bouncing back to school to proudly display her hands, warts and all, boasting to her peers what you had done and said. So thank you again, Roy, for treating one little girl so beautifully. May peace be with you always.

Gwendoline Gracely, Walnut Creek, CA - 11/8/90

to – Roy

In 1950 I was 12 years old. Your act came to Nashville. Your trainer, Mr. Randall, came to Shelbyville, TN. He spent the night, and Trigger put on a show for just me in the barn! I have never forgotten that. I was the luckiest girl in the world!

Flora Barber, Shelbyville, TN - 11/10/90

Ernest Connor riding Dennis and Viola Connor riding Lady
- photo provided by Viola Connor

to – Roy

You and Dale are so much like my husband and I were (until I lost my husband in May.) We had horses, which we loved to ride and mess with, just like you and your Trigger. We enjoyed just being with each other, going to church and taking care of ourselves and our horses. He was 76, and I'm 72. The night my husband passed away he did what he loved to do. We went to mass at 5:30, and at 6:45 or 7 pm we came home, and he got changed into his working clothes, kissed me and went to feed our horses. He'd always walk because that was his exercise. It was about a half mile to where we had our horses. He told me, "I'll be back in a little while," but it was getting dark, so I got in our pickup and drove to the pasture. Then I had to walk, with a flashlight in my hand, through the pasture, calling his name, but no answer. I found him holding onto the rope of his horse, lying flat on his back. That's the way he passed away, doing what he loved to do, his horse at his side. Roy, don't you dare give up when feeling poorly. *You* do what you love to do, for as long as you wish to do it. You'll always have my love and prayers.

Viola Connor, Refugio, TX - 10/1/96

Jean Reedy – photo provided by Jean Reedy

to – Roy

We always look forward to seeing you anytime you make an appearance on any show. We love your songs as well as your movies, and we have the utmost admiration and respect for both you and your lovely leading lady, Dale Evans. You are a perfect couple. I am enclosing a snapshot of myself because I am constantly approached and told how much I resemble Dale. I sure don't mind being told that at all! We are great fans of you both, fans who only want to hear that you are well and happy. All our love and best wishes!

Jean and Robert Reedy, Harrisonburg, VA - 11/8/90

to – Roy

I have so many memories of you that I couldn't to justice to them all. I attended your every movie at the matinee. I was allowed to stay up until 9:30 pm ONLY when it was *your* life on "This is Your Life." You were my fantasy boyfriend as a teen (I'm now 60!) I read and reread Dale's books. I remember how you gestured to her with your fingers during performances to say, "I love you." I've read every book and every article about you, and I still tune in for your guest appearances and comb the papers and magazines for any word of you. I love and respect you.

Patsy Deavers, Newark, OH - 10/7/96

to – Dale

When I found my cat 4 years ago, I named her "Dale" after you. She's a treasure! Thank Heavens for Dale Evans. You made a cowgirl outta' me! I own most of your books, and you are truly an inspiration. You are always in my prayers.

Angie Heaton, Urbana, IL - 12/17/98

Angie Heaton, Dale the Cat and a Cardboard Dale Evans
– photo provided by Angie Heaton

to – Roy

Don't think for one moment that people in this world have forgotten about you and Dale. I have a Roy Rogers pillow on my bed that I have to remove before I go to bed, so you are always in my prayers.

a fan, Honolulu, HI – 10/4/96

Essay

My life began in 1941 in Dothan, Alabama. Times were so different then from the world of now that scarcely any words exist to paint an accurate comparison.

From my earliest memories come thoughts of starting school and longing for Fridays when the agony of lessons and homework would be temporarily suspended for two whole days. In the 1940s, weekends brought the only "outside" family entertainment that was available as far as I knew. On Saturday evenings my family would gather around the furniture-sized, polished-wood radio, carefully tune out some of the static, and listen to *Name That Tune* or the *Grand 'Ole Opry* on clear-channel WSM Radio, originating from the faraway Ryman Auditorium in Nashville. We marveled at how events happening light-years away from us could be heard right in our living room.

While listening to the programs on cold winter nights, we enjoyed "pull candy" made at home from locally produced syrup that had been extracted from sugarcane stalks by mule-powered equipment. On late summer evenings, freshly harvested peanuts, boiled in saltwater and eaten while still hot, accompanied radio sessions. Pull candy, boiled peanuts and radio entertainment were delicacies fit for the tastes of royalty.

Many Sunday afternoons found me sitting next to a radio and listening intently to such adventures as *The Shadow, The Green Hornet, The Whistler, The Long Ranger, Sgt. Preston of the Yukon, The Inner Sanctum,* and *Sky King.* I laughed at the antics of *Amos n' Andy* and *Fibber McGee and Molly.*

On school nights I was to be in bed at 9:00 sharp, and presumably I was to quickly fall asleep. However, there was a radio program that came on at 9:00 that I would not miss for anything. With lights out, I would put the breadbox-sized radio next to my ear and place it and me under the quilt with the volume turned as low as it would go. The program for which I gambled with certain discipline if caught listening to the radio after 9:00 was *Mysterious Traveler,* a

15-minute mystery that started with the forlorn sound of a distant train whistle that made goose bumps crawl over my skin. Why I was never caught red-handed while committing this heinous act of youthful rebellion, only *The Shadow Knows*.

Radio was the high point of entertainment in my life until another medium emerged. At age 7, I became old enough to attend the downtown "picture show" by myself. What? Leaving a seven-year-old child in a theatre all by himself? Yes. This was another time in another world. Children were perfectly safe by themselves in that world, and as far back as I can remember, nothing bad ever happened to any of us.

The picture shows were at the Martin Theatre in downtown Dothan. Getting there for some children meant traveling over dirt roads and brick streets adorned with brass 7-Up® medallions that outlined the pedestrian walkways in the intersections. I still remember the washboard feel of those streets while rolling along on a bicycle.

The absolute greatest thrill of a young child's life at that time was to attend the Saturday afternoon double feature at the picture show. The theatre geared its Saturdays to keeping children mesmerized with twin features plus an ongoing serial and a cartoon. They even had a Movietone newsreel that kept us up to date with what was happening in the world. The serials were adventure stories of favorites such as Lassie, Superman and Captain Marvel, each with a cliffhanger so that you had to see the next Saturday's continuation to find out if the train ran over the rail-tied heroine, or if Lassie found the lost little girl before she froze to death in the snowy mountains.

Admission to the many hours of entertainment was a dime. A large bag of popcorn, a mandatory must-have, was another dime. The scent of popcorn wafting through the theatre was enough to cause withdrawal symptoms if you didn't have a bag of your own. However, this created a big problem to a young cowboy because a nickel was left burning a hole in his jeans pocket. That leftover nickel, from of the "movie-day quarter," caused all of us cowpokes such a dilemma! Sometimes the nickel soft drink won out over a nickel box of delicious Milk Duds®, but no matter what, a kid with a quarter was a happy camper on Saturday afternoons.

The most popular double features were those of cowboys and cowgirls who rode across the silver screen right into the hearts of young boys and girls. The young audience was active and vocal, particularly when the smoke cleared after a serious gunfight and the guys in the white hats were still standing. Strange as it might seem, seldom did anyone get seriously hurt in those shoot-'em-ups. But when it ended, you knew good had won over evil. Those scenes, in stark contrast to today's blood and gore, conveyed the needed message without traumatizing young children.

Those western double features were so popular that occasionally the cowboy stars would make an appearance at the theatre to promote their movies. I recall one Saturday when Bob Steele came to the Martin Theatre and gave us quite a show between double features of his movies. He twirled two pistols on his fingers, occasionally stopping the motion and firing both of them several times to the thrill and delight of all the kids there. Only a cowboy's six-shooter could fire dozens of times in a big shootout without reloading. I still have the 8x10 photograph of Bob Steele that he personally autographed for me in the theatre lobby after the shows ended on that never-to-be-forgotten Saturday.

Although many cowpersons galloped across the gossamer screen of the Martin Theatre, two stars were always the most anticipated by all of the pint-sized film critics—Roy Rogers and Dale Evans. They both had a far-reaching and positive effect on young cowboys and cowgirls, but I only realized later in life what caused the magnetism that drew us back time and again to join them in their movie adventures.

I was in college before I realized that the King of the Cowboys and the Queen of the West were actually a married couple. In their movies, I don't recall any kissing or even handholding. After all, real cowboys did not engage in such icky stuff, knowing going young cowboys would not put up with such silly goings-on from their heroes.

In the 70s, my wife, Elizabeth, and I would rise at 6:00 on Sunday mornings to listen to a radio program called *Country Crossroads*, where Jerry Clower and other show regulars interviewed various Christian celebrities. We were always delighted to hear Roy and Dale on the program telling interesting stories about their lives, or singing a song, or talking about how much they loved the Lord—how refreshing—a couple who lived their Christianity and were not ashamed to publicly acknowledge it.

On one program, I recall Roy talking about an experience he had when a visitor to his museum spotted him there. This large man recognized Roy then ran up and hugged him so hard that he literally lifted Roy right off the floor! A great fan as a young cowpoke, the man was overcome by the unexpected joy of actually getting to meet Roy.

My wife and I always dreamed of one day meeting Roy and Dale. In 1984, we drove to southern California to attend a seminar given at Christian Heritage College by the Institute for Creation Research. When we left El Cajon, we drove to the Roy Rogers Museum in Victorville hoping to see Roy and Dale there. Regretfully, they were not in the museum when we visited, and we were disappointed to not personally meet and hug them ourselves. But we did see Trigger, Buttermilk, Bullet, Nellybelle and many other delights we had seen in their movies. What a grand experience!

Then, when personal items that Roy and Dale had owned began to appear at auction, we thought how nice it would be to have something that belonged to this dear couple we admired so much. A Bible given to Roy and Dale now resides in our library, and my wife is proud to wear some of Dale's jewelry to church and other events. Knowing that Roy and Dale owned these items makes them very special to us.

In writing these words, tears come easily as I think about the closing moments of the shows in which Roy and Dale starred. After all the bad guys had been taken care of, and peace once again reigned on the plains, Roy and Dale would mount their horses and ride off, turning to wave to us as they sang Dale's song, "Happy Trails to you, until we meet again...Happy Trails to you, keep smilin' until then." I cannot write or read these words without inaudibly hearing their sweet voices singing the song.

Well, Roy and Dale, my wife and I did not meet you while you were still here, but we know we will meet someday in Heaven. Forgive us if we rush up and hug you so tight that we lift you right off the streets of gold.

Why are my wife and I so confident that we will meet Roy and Dale one day in that wonderful place called Heaven? Dale answers that question best with these words from her song, "How do I know? Because the Bible tells me so."

Roy and Dale left a great legacy for all of us to cherish and live up to. The love they projected to others and their gentle spirits still speak loudly about the lives they lived and the good examples they set for us to follow. Their legacy lives on in the hearts and lives of countless numbers of people around the globe.

Jerry Akridge, Arab, Alabama, writer, engineer *- 11/24/03*

to – Roy

As a little girl I would never miss an episode of your show. You were a true hero to me, an example of gentle encouragement and kindness and strength that meant so much. I knew if I ever married, the man would need to mirror such traits. Besides my dear daddy, you were my first love. And when I met my husband and learned that he was also a fan of yours and had also planted himself in front of the television just to watch you and Dale go through adventures, and crisis after crisis, only to triumph, I knew I had met my "heavenly partner". Please know that you have blessed so many lives. May you be blessed now and forever with the kind of grace and gentleness that you always demonstrated to others.

Ruth Hungerford, Knoxville, TN -10/ 17/ 96

to – Roy

I think of you when I sit in your restaurant near where I live. I love your roast beef sandwiches. The restaurant will soon close, but that "spot" will always be remembered as Roy's!"

Grace Dexter, Ozone Park, NY – 9/25/96

to – Roy

I know you've probably heard or read this a million times, but it comes from the heart and is true, so here goes. The excitement and happiness you've brought to others like myself can never be measured, but believe me it's out there, in the hearts of the people of this country that feel they "know" you and love you. Roy Rogers, Dale Evans, Trigger, Buttermilk, Nellybelle and Bullet, you bring a smile to my face.

Donna Shirlin, Wayne, MI - 2/2/91

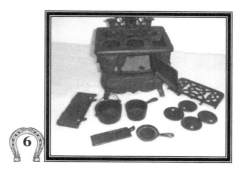

to – Roy

I have your picture in my living room. You're looking great as always!

Marge Frank, Lomira, WI - 11/5/90

to – Dale

"I'm a big fan of both of ya'll. I was so sorry about losing Roy. It really hurt. I have been a big fan of his for a long time. I have two kids now, and they love Roy and Dale, too. I grew up with "Roy and Dale," and Roy will always be my hero. I always wanted to meet you both in person, but I never got to. But I thank you for being you. I'm a true fan forever."

Michael Heltsley, Lewisburg, KY -10/5/98

---

to – Roy

I'm only 22 years old, but I am a big, big fan of yours. My Mom and Uncles told me about all of the happy trails over the years, before my time. I just wanted to say that this crazy world today still needs a hero like you!

Michael Williams, Staten Island, NY - 9/30/96

---

to – Roy

I loved your movies as they had action, music, humor and a little romance, but most importantly, good over evil always won out. I grew up on a ranch, and horses were my best friends. My love for Palominos began with Trigger, and I finally got a Palomino to ride in the later 40s. I always used our best shampoo to wash and braid his tail and mane. I wanted him to be as pretty as your horse. You know, I saw you three or four years ago on a music show, then I saw a picture this week in the news, and I thought, "Wow! Roy Rogers sure looks good year after year!" Ever your fan...

Trudy Greenough, South Lake Tahoe, CA - 9/29/96

1948 – Trudy Greenough riding Terron
- photo provided by Trudy Greenough

to – Roy

When I think of my youth, I think of you and Dale. When I think of happy, wholesome TV, I think you and Dale. When I reflect about "my idols," you are them! What I would give to meet you in person! Please be happy. You're always in my prayers, with love.
Pat Schuler, Amityville, NY - 10/3/96

✦ ✦ ✦ ✦ ✦ ✦ ✦ ✦ ✦

to – Dale

I grew up with Roy as my hero, and he greatly influenced my daily life. I remember that as a child my parents would not let me go to the movies on a Sunday. That was God's day, and they did not believe I should spend it in the movies. Well, we went to Philadelphia to visit my aunt (it was Easter Sunday,) and they had a movie theater around the corner. Roy's movie was playing there, and I begged and begged until they finally gave in a gave me the money to see it. It was wonderful. I have now purchased a lot of Roy's movies on video, and when I watch them, I can return to my childhood. What memories this man gave. In this day there are no heroes for the youth of the country. Roy was special in many ways. There are a lot of acts of kindness that the two of you have done that the public does not even know. Now Roy is in Heaven singing with the angels. God bless you. You have both been class acts, and you gave more than you will ever know. I will always remember and love you both, for you both have a special place in my heart.
Ann Kernechel, Kintnersville, PA - 9/16/98

1957- Paula as Dale Evans and Peter as Roy Rogers – photo provided by Rita Samida

to – Roy & Dale

Our whole family just loves you two people. You were always our favorites. My kids grew up with you (I'm sending a picture.) They were always Roy Rogers and Dale Evans. My girl is now 41, my son is 44, and I am 62. We've watched and admired you all our lives. You are such nice, wonderful people. I think Clint Black looks like you, Roy. His eyes for sure! My husband, John, and I have been married for 45 years and 8 months, and oh how we love you both!

Rita Samida, Oshkosh, WI - 10/25/96

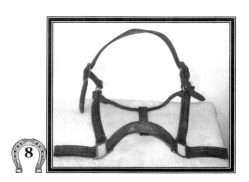

to – Roy and Dale

You are the sun and the moon to generations! And the universe, too!

a fan, MT - undated

to – Dale

I had the pleasure of being at the dedication of your Texas Stars in the Fort Worth Stockyards last year during the Red Steagall Cowboy Gathering. I am a Florida veterinarian born in 1941, so you can tell by my age that I've been a Roy and Dale fan all my life. Roy will be so missed. The loss of the great cowboys is so hard, but they will be remembered. I thought you might like the enclosed poem I wrote as a tribute to Roy Rogers and Gene Autry.

"Rogers and Autry" - by Charles Byron, Jr.

The Lord has called the riders home
The heroes of our youth
They ride and sing on a better range
Than the ones down here on earth

Their horses went before them
A horse don't live that long
So now they're back on Trigger and Champion
Singin' those cowboy songs

So, Roy and Gene, you singin'
cowboys
We still ride for your brands
We hope someday to saddle up
And sing with you again

We still need white-hat heroes
To keep us at our best
Who showed us by example
The Code of the West

Charles Byron, Jr., Margate, FL - 12/7/98

to – Roy

You've been my hero since I was a little girl. When everyone else would watch cartoons, I'd watch you. Reruns of your movies were on at 6:30 Saturday mornings and it was the best reason in the world for getting up in the morning. My admiration for you as an entertainer and person never diminished. You've always set the highest example. Thank you. May sunshine, rainbows, hugs and love always surround you.

Eileen Swingley, Rochelle, IL -11/7/90

to – Dale

My first meeting with Roy and Trigger occurred at the St. Francis theater in San Francisco in the 40s. I sat through 2 movies so I could get to the front row and shake Roy's hand. I had won a ticket for being one of the top newspaper boys for the San Francisco News for that month. I traveled downtown on a bus alone to the theater because my parents were both in the hospital at the time. I thought that was the greatest moment of my life. Years later I was thrilled when I heard that you, Roy and the Sons of the Pioneers were going to meet the Salt Grass Trailriders, of which I was a part, at Spring Branch in 1956. I was again privileged to shake the hand of my hero, Roy Rogers. I also shook hands with you and Pat Brady, although I'm sure you wouldn't remember. I have been extremely lucky to have met both Roy and Gene Autry. Gene rode the entire Saltgrass Trail with us from Brenham to Houston the year before you were there. He was attached to the wagon just in front of the one I was with. He is also a great man. And even though he fell off his horse during the ride, he was still game and got right back on. Those memories will be with me for the rest of my life. I have followed the career of you and Roy since the early days, and there is nobody I have more respect for. I am retired after 42 years as a peace officer in Texas, and I look forward to visiting your museum and Gene Autry's museum on my next trip to California. My wife and I started to go there once, and our vehicle cratered on us just after we crossed the desert. We returned home without getting to see either museum. All Texans love and claim you although you haven't lived here in many years. We believe "once a Texan, always a Texan." We know that you can take people out of Texas, but you can never take the Texas out of them. I do hope to see you again before I am called to meet my maker, so until I do, Happy Trails to you and yours!

Joe Price, Crosby, TX - 2/22/99

to – Dale

We wish to express our gratitude and love to you and Roy, and all the sidekicks who made our generation and upbringing so great. I hope you enjoy my poem.

"Ode to the Cowboy" by Archie Paulson

Whatever happened to Roy and Gene
And the Sons of the Pioneers
Please bring back all the cowboys
That were known throughout the years

The world is taken over
By Ninja Turtles and Star Wars games
Sex and violence and killing
Is all that's to be seen

Imagine what's in our kids' heads
Well, I think it's just a shame
So please bring back our cowboys
Life is not a game

Our kids deserve the best
And good guys always won

My heroes were always cowboys
That put bad guys on the run
Now this new generation's got to have some help
And this means you and I,
And I'm here to tell you that the Lord's a meetin'
With the cowboys in the sky

Can you imagine all the white hats
Sittin' round that table of gold
Just like the words of Tex Ritter's old song,
"It's a sight to behold"

Now if you fellows need any help down here
Well you know who to call
I'd like to be an honorary cowboy
Just because I love you all

Archie and Corene Paulson, Duncanville, TX - 10/15/98

Getting married the Cowboy Way: Archie Paulson's daughter, Trudy, got married on April 9, 2005. The bride and groom celebrated to the strains of "Happy Trails" as guests fired off cap guns in lieu of throwing rice or blowing bubbles. Archie loved his family, all things western, and Roy and Dale. The cap guns were his idea.

2005- Archie Paulson with daughter, Trudy
- photo provided by Trudy

31

to – Roy

Here is a copy of a photo of you, me (age 4, 52 years ago) and my father backstage at the rodeo in New York. I always appreciated you letting me hold your gun as well as your kindness in just being Roy Rogers and being available to fans of all ages. I loved you then. I love you now.

Arth Klau, Highland Park, NJ - 9/30/96

Arth Klau, Roy Rogers, Mr. Klau – photo provided by Arth Klau

Essay

I came up in the "cowboy" movie business under the friendship and guidance of Hoot Gibson, Buck Jones and the great Gene Autry. It was a spectacular time to be a cowboy, and I loved it. I never appeared in a movie with Roy and Dale, but I had the pleasure of knowing them. They were fine, fun people.

Roy loved a challenge, and he loved competition. It was in 1952 when we competed in an offshore boat race to Catalina Island. The race began at the Cabrillo Beach Yacht Club in San Pedro. It was a two-legged race—from the yacht club to the casino on Catalina, then a separate return leg with its own designated start time, back to the yacht club. Roy plotted his course by calculating the wind and sea drift, the boat weight, fuel and body weights, etc. He had it down to a science. Me, I was in the Army, and I had a big, old army tank compass that I just plopped between my legs, and off I went. Roy's calculations got him so off course that I beat him to Catalina by more than an hour. I was kicking back and cooling my heels when he finally showed up, and he wasn't happy!

When it came time to leave on the return leg of the competition, Roy had his game face on, but I still managed to get the jump on him and established a good lead—until I ran out of gas. I was dead in the water, just drifting. I saw Roy coming up on me, and I waved and shouted for him to stop. But old Roy was as happy as a clam. He slowed just long enough to shout, "Get a horse!" before taking off for the finish line, leaving me drifting and bobbing in the ocean. Roy hated to lose. We laughed about day that many times over.

And Dale? She was the sweetest lady you'd ever hope to know. One day, I was in Apple Valley when Roy wasn't feeling up to snuff, and I joined Dale in pursuit of a hot dog for lunch. I pulled out my money to pay, but she just tut-tutted me and said, "You think I can't pay for my own hot dog?" But when she got in her purse, she didn't have any money. She looked at me with a sheepish grin, and said, "Oh, I forgot. I didn't get my allowance yet." We both had a great laugh over that, and I got to buy her a hot dog after all. Roy and Dale were down-to-earth, fun-loving folks. I was grateful to count them as friends.

Dick Jones, Movie and TV Actor

Actor Dick Jones, a silver screen cowboy
- photo provided by Dick Jones

to – Dale

One year ago I sent a photo of Roy and my father, William Lampson, to Roy asking him to please sign and return it so I could give it to my father as a Christmas gift. He did, and what a blessing for my father! You and Roy have always had a special place in my heart. I know that you have been through many trials in this life, but isn't it wonderful to know that you will see your husband and your beautiful children again one day! This past year I heard of so many senseless deaths of babies and little children. Being a mother of 4 beautiful children myself, I can only imagine that the most sorrowful and agonizing pain that a mother or father could experience would be the loss of a child. After hearing of the 5 little girls who climbed into the trunk of a car, became trapped and died, my heart was so heavy. I just cried. That night, I sat at the table and wrote this poem. The words just poured out, and I believe it was from the Lord. I hope this poem can somehow touch the heart of at least one soul in pain.

"Safe in the Shepherd's Arms" by Pam Staples

The eyes of a child
so full of love and trust.
How could we have known
life would be so unjust?
Chubby little fingers
reaching out to take our hand;
How quickly time ran out
in life's hourglass of sand.
Why did it have to happen?
I guess we'll never know.
That little heart we loved so much
is with the angels now.

Oh, Heavenly Father, do you see
my mommy crying so?
My daddy's heart is breaking;
he didn't want me to go.
I wish that I could tell them.
I want to make them see
that I'm so very happy now,
they don't have to cry for me!
I'm not hurting any longer,
I'm not crying anymore.

I felt such peace inside my heart
when I went through the door!
So please, dear Jesus, won't you help
my mommy and daddy see
that I am safe here in your arms;
they don't have to cry for me!

And mommy, it's okay to cry
because you miss me so,
and Daddy, I know that you're so sad
because I had to go
But please, just be sad for a little while
life goes on, don't you see?
And I am safe in the Shepherd's arms,
so please don't cry for me.

Pam Staples, Chino Valley, AZ – 2/1/99

William Lampson and Roy Rogers
- photo provided by Pam Staples

to – Dale

During our third visit to the museum last year, we finally had the honor of meeting you and Roy. I thought you might like to see how you made us smile! God bless each of you.

Dale and Bonnie Miller, Kenosha, WI - 3/ 13/ 99

Bonnie and Dale Miller with Dale Evans and Roy Rogers
- photos provided by Dale and Bonnie Miller

to – Roy

I think all of your movies that I went to every Saturday afternoon a few years back, and it makes me smile! I wish my grandchildren could see them. Those were my "fun" years, and you were, and still are, the greatest cowboy! I'm still your fan and still collect memorabilia of you. I thank you, and I will be thinking of you and Dale always.

Sharon Klug, Escanaba, MI - 10/ 5/ 96

Essay

My brother, Ray Sharpe, and Roy were friends for years. Together, they owned the Dale Jean Corporation Boat Landings in Big Bear Lake, California (named for their wives, Dale and Jean.) Our family has many stories to share— before Roy's wife, Arline, passed on, before any of the children were born or adopted. We remember Arline and loved Dale and all the children as well. We celebrated Roy and Dale's 45th wedding anniversary at Jean Sharpe's home after my brother, Ray, died. The following is derived from a speech I wrote and gave in 2004.

"Growing Up with Roy and Dale" by Tomaline "Tommie" Sharpe Lenox

I remember walking to the neighborhood movie house every Saturday to see Superman, Wonder Woman, The Shadow, cartoons, and best of all, the bigger-than-life, real live person—the King of the Cowboys, Roy Rogers. And King he was—the highest paid western star from 1943-54. He called his fans "buckaroos," serenaded us on 78 records, starred in comics, and entertained us on his shows—first on radio then on television, not to mention the scores of films that hit the Silver Screen. We all had a favorite Roy Rogers flick, especially when he introduced us to the Queen of the West, Dale Evans.

My family met him long before success made him a hero and a household name. My big brother, Ray Sharpe, had fallen in love with Big Bear in 1938 and moved there with his wife, Jean (Sister Jean,) and their children, Jeanie (Sissie) and Raymond III, (Moanie,) my niece and nephew.

The first summer, Ray and the family dug hellgrammites and sold them as bait. Within a year, Ray had build up enough credit to buy lakefront property and opened Pleasure Point Boat landing near Metcalf Bay.

When Roy joined the Sharpe circle of friends, he was married to Arline Wilkins, the woman who baked him lemon pies for what she called his "Swiss Yodel" and who Roy called "the prettiest woman he had ever seen." They met in

Roswell, New Mexico where Roy sang with a group called Cactus Mack and His O Bar O Cowboys. Love at first sight blossomed into marriage in 1936, and Roy later paid the bills with a new group, The Texas Outlaws, then with The Pioneers, who later became the Sons of the Pioneers. Remember Tumbling Tumbleweeds?

By 1942 Roy had embarked on a successful movie career. While filming on location in Big Bear, he decided to go fishing. He chose Pleasure Point, rented a boat from my brother, Ray, and they became fast friends. Ray always called him "Buck," and Roy gave Ray one of his famous hats.

Cedar Lake and Big Bear Valley were favored locations in the area for filming. Jeanie and I used to hike from the landing to Cedar Lake to watch the action. My niece, Sherry Lee, born that year, was a little too young to join us.

Roy loved Big Bear and often vacationed there. Before he bought a cabin for his family, the Sharpes and the Rogers spent many hours in Ray and Jean's cabin near Pleasure Point, feasting on the day's catch—Jean's famous buttermilk, egg and cornmeal-dipped crappie, bluegill, and Roy's favorite, trout.

We learned that Roy was part Cherokee Indian (check the eyes,) and that his family had come to California from Ohio during the depression, looking like something out of Grapes of Wrath, according to Roy. He was Leonard Slye then. Glad he chose a new name for fame!

Roy and Arline adopted their first child, a girl, Cheryl Darlene, in 1942. In 1943, Arline gave birth to Linda Lou. The Rogers family was riding high by 1945—a lucrative film career, two beautiful daughters and a baby on the way. But the mountain top soon became a valley. Six days after Roy Junior was born in 1946, Arline died of an embolism. Roy immediately called Ray, and in the next few months, spent a lot of time in Big Bear where Ray and Jean consoled their broken-hearted friend and his children.

Over time, Roy had many leading ladies—Gale Storm, Marjorie Reynolds, Elyse Knox, Clare Trevor, Adele Mara, and names we've forgotten as the years flew by. But Dale Evans, "Queen of the West," became his good luck charm, and Trigger was soon known as the "Smartest Horse in the West," on the Silver Screen.

Roy and his children spent a lot of time in Big Bear after Arline died. Once in awhile Dale came with him so it didn't come as a surprise when he told Ray and Jean he had asked Dale to marry him. They married in Oklahoma on New Year's Eve, 1947. In 1955, Ray, Jean, Roy and Dale went into business together, buying Gray's landing across the lake for the Dale Jean Corporation.

Everyone in my family has a favorite story about Roy, Dale and Trigger.

My sisters-in-law, Helen and Jean, loved dancing with Roy at Chad's Café in Big Bear. Ray and Jean's trip to Washington DC, while my brother, Eddie, was stationed there, was another highlight. Roy happened to be in New York for a performance at Madison Square Garden and looked up Ray, Jean, Eddie and Helen and gave them choice tickets for the performance.

Jeanie remembers her mom, Jean, barbecuing in the fireplace inside the cabin. One night, with lamb chops spitting on the grill, Roy said, "You're going to cremate them!" "Just wait," Jean smiled. The lamb chops were crisp on the outside but tender and moist on the inside, delicious, like everything Jean cooked. Dale was a good cook, too, and always made hush puppies to serve with Jean's famous trout.

Jean loved to cook for all the Rogers' family, which was growing by leaps and bounds. They rejoiced when Dale gave birth to Robin in 1950 then rode a dark valley when she died in 1952. Robin's memorial service was held on her second birthday, August 26th. Roy said Robin looked like a sleeping angel. Working through her grief, Dale wrote *Angel Unaware* to her baby. After Robin's death, Roy and Dale adopted Sandy, a handicapped boy; Mary Little Doe, part Choctow, Scottish and American; Debbie, a Korean girl, and they became foster parents to Marion, from Scotland. Dale told Roy if they visited the orphanage one more time they would have to buy a hotel. You may remember that Sandy and Debbie had accidental deaths. As she had done for Robin, Dale wrote books to them, too—*Dear Debbie* and *Salute to Sandy*.

Jeanie and her husband, Dick, have lots of memories. Jeanie didn't know Roy was famous when she met him. She was only seven (as I was.) Dick represented Roy's "buckaroo" cowboy fans of Middle America. Dick had lived in Indiana as a child, going every Saturday to the movies to watch his favorite cowboy, then he and his pals would go home to "play cowboy," trying their best to duplicate the movie storyline. So when Dick, a teenager working at Pleasure Point, met Roy, he was awestruck. He followed his idol, admiring his style, his warmth, and his white hat. "It was different than the rest of the cowboy hats," Dick says, "It was really cool, and Roy was the first one to wear one like it."

One day, while the TV show crew was filming a scene with Pat Brady, Dale, and Roy at the landing, the stars were standing on the dock. I don't know if a wave or the wind knocked Pat into the lake, but there he was, splashing around.

Dick also remembers teaching Roy to water ski. Roy had watched him take some turns around the lake. Always the competitor, Roy decided he wanted to try, too. After all, if he could ride Trigger, why not water ski? Only problem was, he couldn't let go of the rope. He never made it to a standing position. Dick had to cut the engine to stop the exercise. Roy blew out his knee with that maneuver. He never ceased to remind Dick, "You remember when I tried to water ski? My knee hurt for the next six years!"

Then there was the time my niece Sherry had an appendicitis attack in Big Bear while Roy was there. He drove with the family to the hospital in San Bernardino, a long way down the mountain. Sherry's condition worsened by the minute, and wasting no time, Roy scooped her up in his arms and carried her into the hospital where she had an emergency appendectomy. Sherry says everyone treated her like a queen after that, especially when Roy came to visit.

Once, when Dale and Roy were visiting in Big Bear, they joined the family to watch their weekly TV show—not an easy feat when the antenna is atop a pine tree. They had just shot the show, and it was their first viewing, too. Dick says, "What a great experience! I'd tell the world Roy's always been my hero, and I don't care who knows it!"

Jeanie and Dick remember Roy and Dale sitting in their living room, petting their little dog, Kizzy. Jeanie asked what they had been doing lately. Always humble, never bragging, Roy and Dale smiled. "We've been in England. Just came home." When asked if they had done anything exciting, Dale added, "Well, we met the Queen and spent the night at Windsor Castle."

My brother-in-law, Bob, has a favorite story, too. Roy was a great enthusiast of hunting raccoons and had a new "coon dog" pup. He decided it was time to try out the puppy's skill. Bob, Roy and Carl Switzer ("Alfalfa" from the "Our Gang" comedies) were trekking through the fields near the Rogers' Chatsworth Ranch when the pup caught the scent. Pups can't read "No Trespassing" signs, and before long, the intrepid crew had gone beyond the point of no return. They split up to try to track the dog that was wailing in the distance. Bob and Roy hid behind separate trees, while Alfalfa scouted up the road. Pretty soon a loud voice yelled, "Who's there? This here's private property. I've got my gun, and I'm a-comin' to git you!" Bob swears it was with a timid squeak that Roy answered, "We're just trying to catch our coon dog. He's just a puppy. We weren't doing anything wrong." Threats and apologies went back and forth for a while before Alfalfa could no longer hold back his laugher. He had been the voice of the "angry landowner" all along and had the pup in tow. But Bob said they hightailed it out of there anyway.

Don and I have favorite memories of Roy, Dale, and their family, too. The first was at Ray and Jean's cabin in Big Bear, sitting around a roaring fire while they regaled us with stories of their life together. Dale said, "After we adopted Sandy, I told Roy, we've got Dusty and Sandy. If we have another boy we'll have to call him Filthy."

That night, my brother played the organ in the living room, and Dale said, "I've just finished a song with Frankie Laine. We've recorded it. Would you like a preview?" Would we ever! We listened and applauded enthusiastically, the very first audience to hear Dale play and sing "Tornado." The next morning, Don piled Dale and her kids into a Pleasure Point boat for a tour of the lake. Everyone had a ball.

I'll never forget the night my niece, Sherry, married Larry Taggart—the reception in the lobby of the La Valencia hotel filled with celebrants, Roy outside looking at the ocean, while Dale and I sat at the grand piano and played duets. What a thrill!

Once, at a Christian conference where Dale was speaking, I brought her greetings from my sister-in-law, Jean. "I just love that woman. She is my sister!" Dale exclaimed. Reading the poem she wrote to Jean is proof of the loving friendship they shared. Dale titled it: To Jean Sharpe, the sister I would have loved to have had."

My last memory of time shared with Dale and Roy happened in Lakeside, in the home where Jean lived after my brother Ray's death. On New Year's Eve weekend, Roy and Dale were in town for a performance and to promote hearing aids. Roy had a new one. The company had set them up in a beautiful suite and reserved spots at a New Year's party. Roy and Dale chose instead to spend their evening, and their 45th anniversary, with Jean, enjoying her wonderful cooking, as always.

Jeanie, Dick, Sherry, Larry, Don and I came, too. Roy and Dale kept us laughing with tales of their lives. Roy said, "Hearing aids, pacemakers—we're all electrical. You know, Dale has a pacemaker now, too," he patted her chest then winked, "I told her if you show me yours, I'll show you mine."

The last years of their lives, Roy and Dale lived in Apple Valley where they established the Roy Rogers – Dale Evans Museum. Much to Dale's dismay, when Trigger died, Roy had him stuffed and put him on exhibit. Dale said, "When you die, we'll put you on Trigger." Roy answered, "That's OK, just make sure I'm smiling!"

Then there was the time Dick's grandkids gave him a brand new cowboy hat. (Dick isn't "Grandpa," he's "Cowboy.") He asked Roy how he formed his hat to the unique shape that only Roy sported, and Roy said, "Let me shape it for you. Where's your shower?" He turned the water up high, and filled Dick's new hat to the brim with hot water. Dick almost fainted. "My new hat!" Roy grinned and began molding the brim to the distinctive shape of his own hat. He worked about twenty minutes, pulling it this way and that, then satisfied, tied it in place with a scarf. The result was perfect.

On their last trip to Lakeside to see Jean and visit with other friends in Coronado, they were in town so Dale could deliver a scheduled speech at a local church. She wanted Roy to sing with her to close the program. At first he said "no," then agreed. The man who was so cool on the screen and with friends was tongue-tied in public.

Before Dale introduced Roy, she shared a short film Roy had made singing with Clint Black, who wore a black hat. Dale told the crowd, "I want you to meet a friend of mine. He's my favorite cowboy, the good guy in the white hat." Roy joined Dale on stage to sing "Happy Trails." He missed cues, didn't sing at the right time and afterwards told Dale he sounded terrible. Her reply? "Honey, you could sound like a toad and people would love you."

Dick and Jeanie think maybe that trip was a journey to say goodbye to old friends. Illness followed, and two years later, Roy died. Among the flowers at his memorial stood a tall pole topped with Roy's white hat, symbolic of the man, the good guy, the King of the Cowboys.

Dale wrote, "Roy Rogers was a wonderful human being. What a blessing to have shared my life with him for almost 51 years. To say I will miss him is a gross understatement. He was truly the King of the Cowboys in my life. He loved his God, his country and his family. God bless him. He was a real hero to thousands of people, and thank you, God, for the years we had together."

Speaking of hats, when my brother, Ray, died, Dick inherited one of Roy's hats, with the perfect brim and Roy's sweat by his name on the inside band.

Roy Jr. moved the Roy Rogers – Dale Evans Museum to Branson, Missouri, home of country singers and scores of fans who remember their performances, their movies, their books, and their songs, like Dale's "The Bible Tells Me So." Their Christian faith played a tremendous part through all the mountains and valleys in their lives.

Roy said the "Cowboy's Prayer" at all his Riders' Club meetings: *"Oh Lord, I reckon I'm not much by myself. I fail to do a lot of things I ought to do. But Lord, when the trails are steep and the passes high, help me ride it straight the whole way through. And when in the falling dusk I get the final call, I do not care how many flowers they send. Above all else the happiest trail would be for you to say to me, "Let's ride my friend."*

When we remember Roy and Dale, this song will always be with us:
"Happy Trails to you, until we meet again
Happy Trails to you, keep smiling until then
Who cares about the clouds if we're together
Just sing a song and bring the sunny weather
Happy Trails to you, 'til we meet again."

Our memories of Roy and Dale are as new today as when we shared time with them. They were dear, down to earth, spirit filled, funny and fun, caring and compassionate. Knowing them has been a gift.

Clockwise: Roy Rogers, Dick Medenwald, Jean Sharpe, baby Rick Medenwald, Jeannie Sharpe Medenwald
– photo provided by Tomaline "Tommie" Sharpe Lenox with permission from Dick and Jeannie Medenwald

"To Jean Sharpe, the Sister I Would Love to Have Had" was written by Dale Evans in 1951 and sent to her friend, Jean Sharpe. Many years later Dale's poem was shared at Jean's memorial service. The poem is provided with permission from Jeanie and Dick Medenwald (Jean and Ray's daughter and son-in-law.)

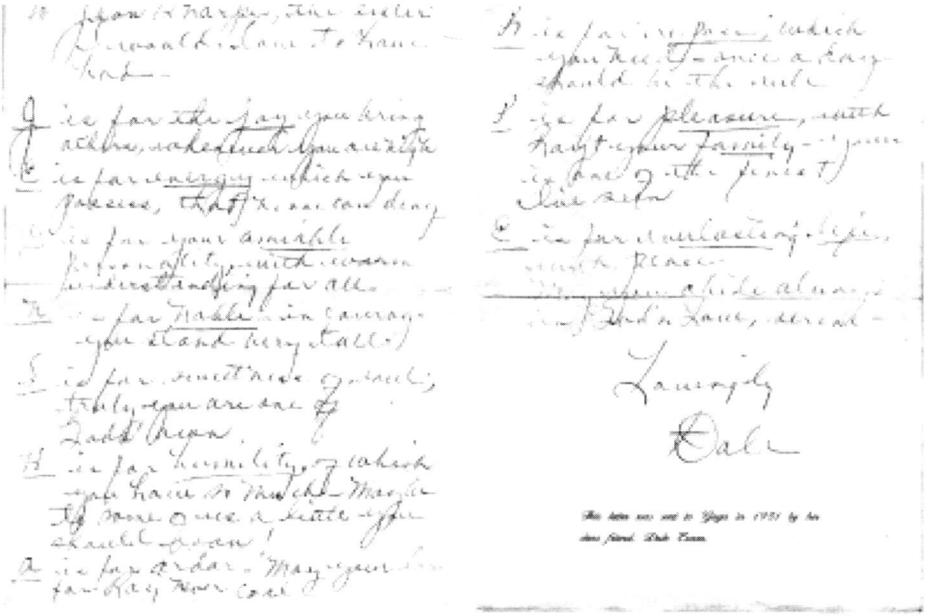

1951 handwritten poem from Dale Evans to Jean Sharpe

"To Jean Sharpe, the Sister I Would Love to Have Had"

by Dale Evans

J is for the joy you bring others, whenever you are nigh
E is for the energy you possess, that no one can deny
A is for your amiable personality, with warm understanding for all
N is for noble in courage; you stand very tall

S is for sweetness of soul, truly you are one of God's own
H is for humility, of which you have much—maybe to some of us a little
you should loan!
A is for ardor, may your love for Ray never cease
R is for repose, which you need—once a day should be the rule
P is for pleasure, with Ray and your family—yours is one of the finest I've seen
E is for everlasting life with peace. May you always abide in God's love serene.

Lovingly,

Dale

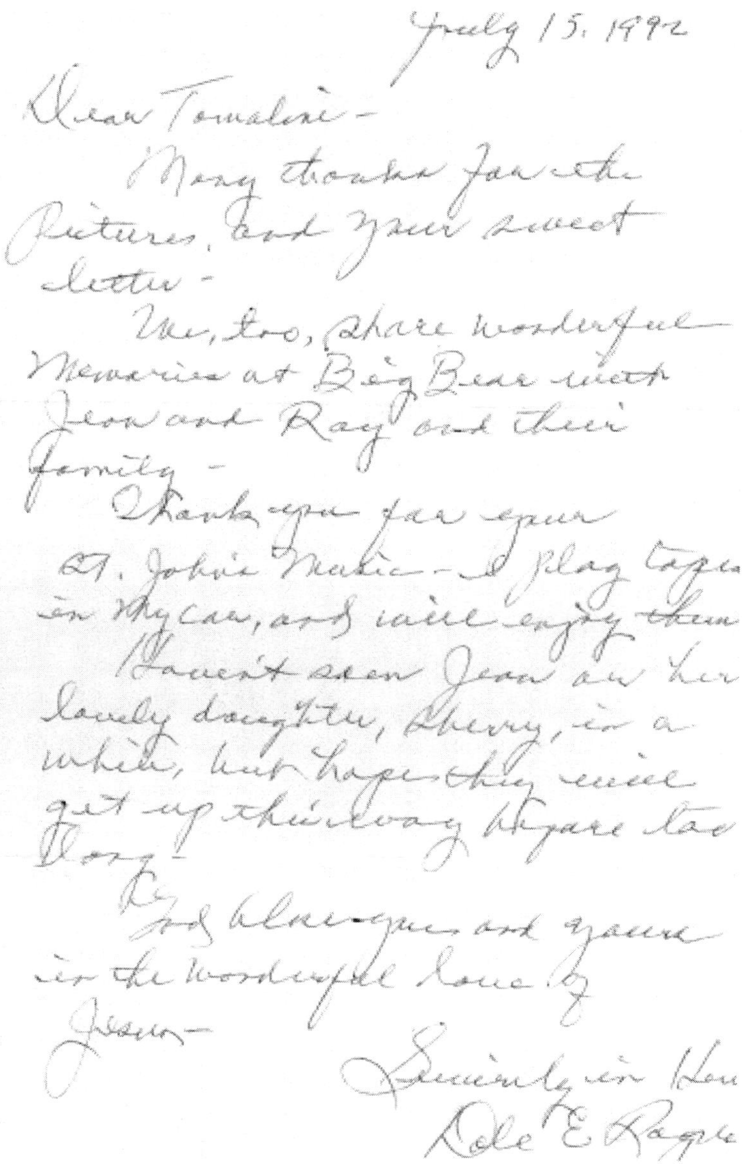

July 15, 1992

Dear Tomaline —

Many thanks for the pictures, and your sweet letter —

We, too, share wonderful memories at Big Bear with Jean and Ray and their family —

Thank you for your St. John's music — I play them in my car, and will enjoy them.

Haven't seen Jean or her lovely daughter, Sherry, in a while, but hope they will get up this way before too long!

God bless you and yours in the wonderful love of Jesus —

Sincerely in Him
Dale E. Rogers

July 15, 1992 Letter from Dale Written to Tomaline "Tommie" Lenox

The Rogers Family clockwise from top: Cheryl, Linda, Sandy, Dale, Mary Little Doe, Roy, Roy "Dusty" Jr.
– photo provided by Tomaline "Tommie" Sharpe Lenox

Tomaline "Tommie" Sharpe Lenox, El Cajon, CA

Author of *Crying in the Wilderness: A Voice for America's Children*

to – Roy

     A few months ago our local club put out a flyer which read: Roy Rogers and the Delta Rhythm Kings. In a town of 25,000, I thought this was too good to be true, but I hurried to buy tickets to see Roy Rogers! I didn't ask anyone if it was the *real* Roy Rogers. Although it said "rhythm and blues dance concert," I convinced myself that you may have had friends or relatives in the area, and you were going to make a guest appearance. I couldn't believe I was going to see *the* Roy Rogers. At 46, I'm still a believer. A few days before the gig, an

> Deborah Lazio Productions &
> The International Beer Garden
> Present...
>
> ### Saturday, July 21
>
> Rhythm & Blues Dance Concert
>
> # Roy Rogers
> ## & The Delta Rhythm Kings
>
> **Show 9:30/Doors 8:30**
> **Tickets $8**
> All Ages Welcome
>
> Concert Information Line: 822-0870
>
> **International Beer Garden**
> **856 Tenth Street • Arcata**
>
> 00058

article was in the local paper talking about Roy Rogers, "a namesake," guitarist from San Francisco. I was so disappointed. I called the club to voice how I felt. They thought I was pretty funny, and no refund to boot. Some of my friends are still laughing at me, but I don't care. I believed. If only...
Shiela Daggs, Eureka, CA - 11/17/90

to – Dale

     Roy's death was a personal loss, as I am one of his "buckaroos." He was a true hero in every sense of the word. Roy, Gene, Hoppy and the Lone Ranger fought against evil and did so without a lot of blood and guts. It's sad that children today do not have such heroes to look up to. Saturday morning TV is now full of animated characters, not real people. Once, our local theater held a voting contest to elect the *real* "King of the Cowboys" and we all know who won—Roy, of course! I had the biggest crush on Roy, and at age five I was so jealous when you married him. But then I decided you were not so bad after all. As a matter of fact, you had to be some kind of special for Roy to want you for his life partner. The world lost someone very special the day Roy died, but maybe the Lord needed some good music and fine yodeling in Heaven. No one can take his place. Roy was truly the King of the Cowboys—truly a hero.
Cherry Thrash, Crystal River, FL - 7/22/98

to – Roy

You have given me so many happy memories. As a small boy you entertained me and inspired me to be honest, moral and dependable. You definitely had a great influence on my life. If we had more people like you in this old world, it would truly be a better place to live. You are a true HERO! God bless you and keep you!

Judge Fred Nutt, Justice of the Peace, Paris, TX - 11/12/90

Judge Fred Nutt
Justice of the Peace

Prec. 5 Place 2 - Lamar County - Tx.

**Judge Nutt passed away on January 20, 1996, and his love for his silver screen heroes, Roy Rogers and Gene Autry, was remembered even in his memorial. His long-time secretary, Jill Hart relates: "Judge Fred Nutt was a Justice of the Peace in Lamar Co. TX for 18 yrs. (1978 – 1996.) He was a big fan of Gene Autry, Smiley Burnett, Roy Rogers, Dale Evans and cowboy music. The judge always arrived for work singing "I'm Back in the Saddle Again" and left for the day singing "Happy Trails." He was also known to strike up a chorus of "Happy Trails" after pronouncing a couple husband and wife. Judge Nutt kept the "singing cowboy era" alive during his lifetime, and it seems like you can still hear his faint yodel of the "Cattle Call" in the empty halls of the courthouse."

Judge Nutt's daughter, Kathy Nutt Johnson, added: Roy, Dale and Gene were such a huge influence, and role models, to my dad. He was one of their biggest fans, and he loved them all dearly. They meant so much to his life, and they were instrumental in the way he led his life.

to – Roy

You should know that I am a black man in his late forties. But you must also know that you are one of my all-time heroes. This may or may not come as a total surprise to you, but you are still a hero and thought fondly of by hundreds of thousands of black men over 40. In the 1940's and '50's, cowboy movies were the rage for young, impressionable boys. There were always heated discussions as who was the number <u>two</u> favorite, the Durango Kid, Lash LaRue, Allan "Rocky" Lane, Randolph Scott, and yes, even John Wayne. My point is that there was never a discussion as to who was number <u>one</u> – no discussion, just total agreement – Roy Rogers. You, Roy Rogers, impacted a whole host of young black boys in a positive way. We always wanted to be that hero you were to us, protect the helpless, look out for the elderly and weaker persons. You instill a sense of honesty and integrity in us. Shucks, Roy Rogers wouldn't steal, so we didn't. Roy Rogers didn't curse, so we didn't. You gave us a "role model" of exemplary behavior, but still allowed us to be tough, yet nice and caring. We all felt that if we did good deeds, good things would happen to us. Thank you, Roy. Not only were you the "ideal" and "natural" person on the screen, but in subsequent life, you are still setting the example – good father, strong and smiling warm person. You did a lot for me, and millions of others like me. God bless.

J.T., OH - 11/9/90

51

I'm a child of the 1950s, and early television hooked me as soon as my family acquired its first little black and white model. I remember sticking a plastic sheet onto the TV monitor to turn black-and-white into "color" (I don't remember quite how that worked.) I loved *Pinky Lee, Ding-Dong Schoolhouse*, and *Buffalo Bob & Howdy Doody*. Most of all I remember Roy Rogers and Dale Evans, with their sidekick Pat Brady and the jeep NellyBelle. I remember Buttermilk, Trigger and Bullet, too. When I was four years old, I received a Dale Evans cowgirl costume for my birthday. I was in Heaven! There was a little fringed vest and a holster with a toy gun, and a cowgirl's hat! My best friend was a little boy who lived down the street, Terry Jordan. He also had a cowboy outfit, with chaps and a hat. We played endlessly together, on long summer afternoons and into the late autumn before snow forced us into snowsuits and galoshes. Alleyways behind neighborhood garages turned into secret passageways where we could ambush the "bad guys." Bushes and trees gave us hiding places from "non-friendly scoundrels." Our buddies, the Reidy brothers (Jimmy and Tommy,) often joined us for posse duty. Best of all, we could sit in front of the television for half an hour of mystical communion with Roy and Dale, fulfilling our fantasies and providing endless storylines for the next afternoon's adventures. We never missed an episode. Sadly, when we were old enough to go to school, Terry and I grew apart. We went to different schools: he to the Catholic parish school and I to the public school on the corner. In a couple of years my family moved to the suburbs and I never saw Terry again. My cowgirl outfit was put away and I never saw it again either. But I'll always have a little Dale in me, ready to ride the range whenever the call comes!

Barbara Bell, Syracuse, NY
Collector, Writer, and Proprietor of thewisecollector.com

to – Dale

We have a daughter in Lima, Peru, married to a Peruvian, and just for fun I asked him if he had ever heard of Roy Rogers. He is "big city" and not the least bit interested in the West, horses, or anything of that nature, besides being one of the "younger generation." But he knew who Roy Rogers was. He said everybody did down there! Their little daughter speaks only Spanish, and because she was fascinated with Roy and Trigger, I taught her Stan Corliss' "Roy Rogers" song. She loved it, and it was a great icebreaker for us both. We have another daughter in Vancouver, and she tells us that the nightclubs play "Happy Trails" when they are shutting down for the night. Thought you'd get a smile from that. With such good cassettes, CDs and videos available, you and Roy become part of our own families and stay forever young. When Roy died, there was real grief in our family. We would just like you to know that we think of you these days and wish you all the best.

Elizabeth McDonald, Chase, B.C., Canada - 12/9/98

to – Roy

You are a national treasure and admired by millions. May God continue to bless you!

Earl Wilkins, Windsor, VA - 10/29/90

to – Roy

You have been my idol since I was a kid, and that was way back in the 40s! I've always been crazy about horses and cowboys and anything western. I want to tell you what happened to me back in 1973. Ten years prior to that I had lost my Palomino horse that I loved so much. Needless to say, I was heartbroken and very depressed. The depression worsened, and I was in and out of hospitals, trying all kinds of medicine, none of which helped. Finally, the doctor asked my husband if he could think of anything that would make me want to live. My husband said, "A horse. If that doesn't do it, nothing will." A few days after that, a van drove up to our house and unloaded a beautiful sorrel and white paint mare. I couldn't believe it. I started crying tears of joy, then my husband and daughter were crying, too! From that time on, I began to improve. I rode Dolly daily, and she gave me back my life. It brought me out of the depression and gave me a reason to live. I had Dolly for 18 years. She died of old age at 30. I'll always thank my husband and Dolly for saving my life. Roy, if you are well enough to get on a horse, even if you have to just sit there, it might help you, too. I still ride (at 69) whenever I get a chance. You and Dale have contributed so much to the motion picture industry and to the youth of this country. You made good, clean family movies that taught honesty and respect, so little of what we see today. I treasure the many clippings and pictures of you and Dale that I've saved over the years. I did see you both in person years ago when you appeared at the Vermont State Fair in Rutland, Vermont. In fact, I got to shake Dale's hand but was unable to get to you. I was very disappointed. We all love you and are rooting for you. You see, I know what illness can do to a person. My husband of 51 years is trying to walk again after spending 6 months in the hospital with a punctured colon. He's had open-heart surgery, two abdominal aneurysms and still has another inoperable one. He is living on borrowed time, and he knows it. It is very stressful for me, but when it gets too bad, I bury myself in a good western book, read the Bible, or look through the scrapbook I have of you and once again dream of the West. It helps me to carry on. God bless and you keep you both always.

Lorraine Dudley, Crown Point, NY - 10/7/96

THE GOVERNOR OF THE STATE OF FLORIDA

LAWTON CHILES

October 7, 1996

to – Roy

I sincerely hope this letter finds you having a good day. You have contributed many years of your life to entertaining others through the motion picture and television industry. You have been a great inspiration to millions, and I know you have touched many lives by sharing your wisdom and experience. My best wishes are sent for added strength each day. With kind regards, I am

Lawton Chiles, Governor of the State of Florida

Sincerely,

LAWTON CHILES

Former Florida Governor Lawton Chiles
- photos and quote provided with permission by the Lawton Chiles Foundation

55

to – Roy

I have a song for you, and I've always wanted you to hear it. I believe if kids today had heroes like you to look up too, we wouldn't have all the gang activity, carjackings, or drive-by shootings that we have today. I still recall, as a kid, how we could hardly wait for that Saturday afternoon matinee down at the old El Lasso Theatre. Every kid in town was there to see Roy Rogers, Dale Evans, Gabby Hayes, Bullet and Pat Brady run the bad guys out of town. This old cowpoke's a whole lot bigger, but you know what? I still miss old Trigger! You meant so much, and you can rest assured that everyone is praying for you. And when you feel better, get your exercise by walking down to the studio and recording "Trudy" for me. Then Gene won't be able to hold Rudolph over your head anymore! Roy, I want you to know. I'll remember you always.

"Trudy the Long-Ear Reindeer" by Charles H. Norman

There's something cooking in
Santa's workshop
It's gonna be a big surprise
He's hiding something behind those
whiskers
You can tell by the twinkle in his
eyes

He's found a solution to any
intrusion
As he circles the world in his sleigh
Now Trudy the long-ear reindeer
Will be on every child's lips today

Trudy, you're a special reindeer
And, with your great big ears

You could help old Santa deliver
So much Christmas cheer

Now you might not be
Just e-x-a-c-t-l-y
The way that reindeer
Ought to be
But it does appear with your radar
ears
You can "see" what Santa cannot
see

Now children won't have to worry
And Santa won't have to fear
For Trudy the long-ear reindeer
Will guide Santa's sleigh this year

And, Roy, I also wanted to share my poem about the precious, fleeting moments of childhood. I hope you like it.

"Stick Horses, Teddy Bears and Clay" by Charles H. Norman

Daddy, you said
you'd take me fishing
If you could only find
the time
You promised we'd
go camping
But I guess it slipped
your mind.

But that's alright, Daddy
I know you'll find some time to play
With me, my stick horse, Teddy
Bear, and
My old border collie, Clay

Now Daddy, I know you need your
rest
You have to work so hard and all,
But you know when you get ready
I'll come running when you call

So don't you worry about me, Daddy
I won't get in your way
I'll just ride off to greener pastures
On my stick horse—with Teddy Bear
and Clay

Now that old storybook's still open
Upstairs beside my bed
Tonight if you tuck me in
There's a story to be read

But, Daddy, I can understand
When you say "some other day"
It might wake up my stick horse,
Teddy Bear,, or Clay

Now it won't be much longer, Daddy
I won't be here to bother you
For I'll just ride my old stick horse
Off into the blue

And, Daddy, I know
you mean well
In all you do and
say
In that there'll
always be a place
For stick horses,
Teddy Bears, and
Clay

Now Daddy, I know you don't have
the time
To hear what I've got to say
To brush away my teardrops
Or help me when I pray

But that will be alright, you know
It's not as lonely as it seems
For each night you ride off with me
On my stick horse...in my dreams

Charles H. Norman, Uvalde, TX - 9/30/96

to – Roy

I briefly shook your hand once, but it could have been even better. In 1991 I had the opportunity to speak with you and Dale at the Golden Boot awards, but I was too nervous to approach you as everyone else seemed comfortable in doing. That's truly a regret. However, I have had the pleasure of writing to you on numerous occasions, and I am ever grateful for the autographed photo you sent to me. I wish you the best always.

Erik Madden, New York, NY – 11/2/90

Roy and Dale photo autographed to Erik Madden
- photo provided by Erik Madden

to – Roy

I believe that you were my first real hero. I remember in 1948 when I was 10 years old that you got a standing ovation from the audience in Mt. Clemens, Michigan. This was at one of your movies at the Macomb Theater. It was wonderful. I remember Gabby Hayes ("You're durn-tootin!) (Yesirreee, Bob!) and Andy Devine, and of course, Dale Evans. In my younger years I had a bit of a crush on her. I heard that you are not a tall man. Neither am I. But you are tall-in-the-saddle to me. I remember you on the radio, and one time in one of your stories (called "adventures" on the radio,) you threatened an unruly crowd with Trigger. Even as a kid I knew that Roy Rogers and Trigger would never hurt a crowd. You were way above that! I always love it when you and Dale sang "Happy Trails to You." Roy, I hope you feel as good as you can for as long as you want. Love forever.

Jim Henriksen, Mt. Clemens, MI - 9/30/96

Meeting the Queen of the West

She was a vision in purple that summer day in 1999 in Victorville, California. Dale Evans graciously agreed to an interview with Michelle Freedman and me for our book, *How the West Was Worn*. We peppered her with questions about her career and her fabulous wardrobe, mostly created by the legendary Nudie. Though she'd suffered a stroke three years earlier, her memory was keen: she remembered details going back half a century. Dale was particularly fond of a kelly-green cowgirl outfit designed in the '40s by another great rodeo tailor, Nathan Turk, which was decorated with steer heads, a salute to Texas where she was born. Sitting there chatting with us, Dale was resplendent in an outfit designed by Nudie in the 1950s. She smiled as she reminisced about the sparkling show clothes she and Roy wore during their Madison Square Garden performances.

I asked about "Happy Trails," her classic composition that became the couple's theme song. She began writing tunes as a child, it turned out. Being a songwriter was one of many talents she wanted to pursue as a young girl. She left home as a teenager, determined to make it as an entertainer. The odds were not in her favor. She came of age during a time when women were expected to stay home, keep house and raise children. But Dale sought a career in Memphis, Louisville, Chicago, and finally Hollywood. Though she struggled for years, she never gave up her dreams.

So many of us have been inspired by Dale's courage, artistry and spunk. She paved the way for generations of gals who wanted to make it as singers, writers and actors. The Dixie Chicks spoke for all of us when they sang, "Thank Heavens for Dale Evans!"

Holly George-Warren, award-winning author of multiple books including *How the West Was Worn, Public Cowboy No. 1: The Life and Times of Gene Autry, Cowboy! How Hollywood Invented the Wild West* and *Honky-Tonk Heroes and Hillbilly Angels: The Pioneers of Country & Western Music*

Holly George-Warren and Dale Evans
- photo provided by Holly George-Warren

Dale's Nathan Turk-designed steer-head outfit modeled by Western singer and artist,
Kimberly Bell
- photos provided by Tricia Spencer

to – Roy

I am a 63-year-old mother of 5 and grandmother of 10 who shook hands with you and Dale at the downtown Indianapolis, Indiana Sears Roebuck store when I was 10 or 11 years old, and I will never forget shaking hands with my hero—Roy Rogers! And Trigger bowed for me, too! I sure didn't want to wash my hand after that, but Mother made me. When we went to southern Indiana to see our cousins I really bragged about seeing you. It was such a big thrill in my life. I got to shake hands with my hero, my role model, an honest American and a straight-shooter, so, Roy, stay with us. We need you! Believe me I know that as we get older we slow down some, but we are still useful and have accumulated knowledge about lots of things to share with our children, grandchildren and others. We know how to respect ourselves as well as others, and that's saying a lot in this day because respect for the most part has gone by the wayside. Family, morals, God, compassion, togetherness, understanding, thoughtfulness, etc.—these are what we were taught when I was growing up— true values. I remember that when you made a movie you always got the bad guy, but you didn't kill him. You brought him to jail, and he had a fair trial. You didn't slaughter him in the street as most of the movies today do, and there was no bed hopping or tongue swallowing as there is today. You made good, believable, wholesome, clean movies for us, and we really appreciate you and Dale for your contribution to our upbringing. In the movies you depicted a good, clean image, and I truly believe that's they way you are in real life. When God made you, he really did throw away the mold. God bless and Happy Trails!
Kathryn Alcock, Indianapolis, IN - 10/8/96

13

Norma Clark and Roy Rogers

– photo provided by Norma Clark

to – Roy

Forgive us for calling you "Uncle", but that's how we affectionately think of you. It seems like we've known you forever, and that's because you reached us, and touched us, when we were just kids. All those Saturday matinees we looked forward to seeing you and Dale (and Trigger) in those dark theaters, knowing you as trusted friends. Watching you, without fail, do the right thing: beat up the bad guys, rescue whoever was hanging from the cliff, save the ranch from that Evil Eye with the long mustache, or get back the stolen money. You did it all in a cloud of dust with guns a-blazing and even sang us a song or two along the way. And then you did it all over again, for our kids, on morning TV. A lot of gray has crept into our lives over the years, but that makes us ever more grateful for the memory of those simpler days when things were black and white, right or wrong, when we wore white hats and stood tall, like our heroes – like you. Of course, admiring someone on the silver screen is different than real life. However, we had the good fortune of meeting you at your museum in Victorville a few years back, and you did not fail us. Your warmth, graciousness and the generosity of your nature were so apparent and sincere that we came away seeing the real you standing even taller than the screen image. Happily we captured that warmth in a photo. It is a treasured memento. We are people you don't even know but you came into our lives when we were young and you never left. It should give you a great rush of pride to know that you visited our minds and our hearts when we were first learning about values, and we grew up better human beings for it. But that's what heroes do. With deep gratitude and affection we wish you and Dale good health and well-earned happiness.

Norma and Guy Clark, Huntington Beach, CA -10/1/96

to – Roy

THEN (10/1/96): While my apples cook on the stove on their way to becoming applesauce, I will tell you what you've always meant to me. When I was a little girl living in a small town, I would mow my folks' lawn to earn 25 cents for the afternoon movie, and, Roy, when your sweet, handsome self would

photo of and provided by
Kathy Jarosinski

appear on the BIG screen, it was the thrill and adventure of my little life. You entertained all us kids, freely giving your talent and your gifts to the world. I thank you for that. Maybe I was 7 years old the August-September that you came to Toronto, Canada to perform at the C.N.E. (Canadian National Exhibition.) Well, my daddy knew what a big fan of you I was, and he surprised me with a train trip to Toronto to see you in person. It was a dream come true. When the M.C. asked you when your birthday was and you said

November 5th, I jumped up and screamed, "THAT'S MY BIRTHDAY, TOO!" My daddy chuckled, and more recently, so does my husband when I tell this story. You thrilled me with your dazzling horsemanship, your singing, yodeling, tender love and care of Dale, and, Roy, your good values. You were, and are, something wonderful.

NOW (7/6/11): Roy was the image of an older brother—healthy, active, responsible, fair, and he loved animals and helped kids and elders. Each show episode had the HUGE enjoyable element of music, with camaraderie and the sweet comforting sounds of singing and guitar-playing that sent out the message that "all is well." Everything a child needed was there. Later in life I realized that Roy and Dale weren't simply acting their do-good roles. They *lived* that way. Wouldn't it be wonderful if we all lived that way?
Kathy Marquis Jarosinski, Lumby, B.C., Canada – 10/1/96

---

to – Roy

You and Dale and Trigger are an American institution! God bless you.
a fan, TX – 12/18/90

to – Roy

Imagine *me* writing to *the* Roy Rogers just as if he were a member of my family! To tell you the truth, Roy, I've always loved you like family. Do you know what? I always said Roy Rogers was my boyfriend when I was growing up. But I really meant you were my *good friend*. I've never forgotten you, Roy! And I'll bet that when we get to Heaven you'll still be the King of the Cowboys, 'cause there's going to be horses in Heaven, Roy. I just know it! I have two horses. My mare, Dusty (no offense – ha!) is 24 years old and three quarter Arabian. I've had her 21 years. She is a member of the family and a wonderful horse! I asked God to give me one more colt from her so that if something happened, I'd have a part of her still. Three years ago, with the vet's okay, He did, and she gave me a beautiful Appaloosa colt. I remember when you and Dale got married. I love her, too, and I love Trigger and Bullet. My son's first pony was Trigger, and my oldest granddaughter had a Trigger, too. Everyone at work remembers Roy Rogers, and when I ask, they all say, "Oh yes! I've always loved Roy Rogers!" I was born in Creston, Iowa. Guess you never heard of that place. I'm 63 years old, but I'm like you, Roy. I don't look or feel it! I sure wish I lived closer. There's nothing I would love more than to talk to you and Dale face to face. My love and Happy Trails to you! May the good Lord bless you real good! I remember the day they announced on the radio that you and Dale got saved. I was so excited! Actually, it was Sunday night, and I stayed home from church. I guess I didn't feel well. Anyway I was alone and decided to make a peach pie out of a can of peaches. It turned out awful! I guess I missed the part in the recipe that said "drain the peaches." That pie was a mess! (I was 14 at the time I think.) I put a sign on my pie that read: "There will be no disappointments in Heaven!" I went to bed leaving it for the family when they came home. They laughed and said the taste was all that mattered and it was good. ha ha! It wasn't! Well, bye for now. Love ya! See you here, or there, or in the air! PS. My name is French, but I'm really Irish. I know. Too funny. And one more thing. May the Good Lord take a liken' to ya!

LaVona Jarvis, Springfield, IL -10/26/96

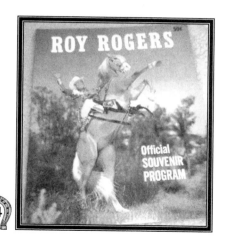

14

to – Roy

I've been wanting to write to you for years. I think of you all the time. Remember when we used to play games on the grocery corner just east of your grandparent's house on Front Street and Bind Street, by Barr's Grocery Corner? Well, we moved from Portsmouth, around 1915 or so, to Dayton, Ohio. When my folks passed away we moved to Englewood, Ohio and have been here ever since. I think of you and would try to get to see you when you came to areas close by, but I can't drive too far, just locally. My right eye was put out by a stroke in 1965, and I can't see too good. I remember your mother and father when they used to visit your grandparents on Front Street. My grandparents, the Gradys, lived across the street from them. Tell Dale about me, that I knew you when. I have been married since 1929—61 years. I am 83 years old, and my wife is 81. I am your old friend.

Harold Danes, Englewood, OH -11/19/90

---

to – Roy

"I'm only 22 years old but even I know you and your wife are living legends!

D.G., IL - 11/6/90

to – Roy and Dale

THEN (10/3/96): I'm not much at writing letters, and as many times as I thought of writing you in the past, hearing of your recent hospital stay made me knock down the rails and get out of the corral. It really gave me a burr under the saddle to hear this, for we need Roy and Dale on the trail every day. Heroes come and go through one's lifetime, but Roy, I'm 60 years old, and you've been my #1 hero for that long. My two brothers and I recall the happiest years of our lives when we used to walk down the country road in Colorado to town with a quarter in our pockets to watch you and Dale on the screen. It was about 1950 when you appeared at Hughes Stadium in Sacramento. My mother, who was as big a fan as us young brothers, took us to see you. I recall my younger brother being lucky enough to fight his way to the arena edge to touch your hand as you rode Trigger around the arena. He tripped all the way back to his seat staring at his hand, and Mom couldn't get him to wash it for two days. As I said, my mother was a great fan also, and I recall sitting next to her during one of your movies. My leg was black and blue for a few days afterward from her beating on it and yelling, "Come on Roy! Come on Roy!" when you were after the bad guys. My younger brother claims that he still has a small piece of deer hide given him by a taxidermist who did some work for you. We lived next to this gentleman in Loomis, California during the 50s. Roy, I just wanted to write a short note to you and Dale to wish you well, and here I am rambling on, but there are just so many memories pushing to the surface. My generation has been so fortunate to have you as role models. Your inspirations will live forever. This is the only letter I've ever written to a movie star, hero or public figure. By the way, we loved the video you made with Clint Black. It is so great. I got a big lump in my throat while watching it because of the pride I felt just having you in our lives. Thanks for everything! May you always have Happy Trails and we love you both!

NOW (6/29/11): When we lost Roy, Dale, Trigger, Buttermilk and Bullet, we lost a big piece of the romance of the Old West. Roy and Dale's wholesome and heart-warming movies and appearances left a person with a sense of pride, as if they were a part of your own family. I'm 75 years old now, and I still wake up at 4:00 am to watch a Roy Rogers movie on the western channel. What great role models Roy and Dale have been. I was elated when Roy Jr. (Dusty) and his son, Dustin, were on the RFD TV channel hosting the "Happy Trails Theater." It was like having a piece of Roy still with us. I'm very disappointed that the show is no longer airing. I'm so happy to see, however, that they are continuing Roy's legacy. We're very proud of them. We all have childhood memories of Roy and Dale in our lives, like picking lilies from the pond and selling enough of them to make a quarter to go see the latest Roy Rogers movie. Losing Roy and Dale left a big void in this world, but God bless them for the memories we inherited from them.

Wayne Runnestrand, Roseville, CA – 10/3/96

to – Roy

You've always meant so much to me, and I learned volumes from your TV show. I've taped many of your westerns and also have cassettes of you singing. I love your voice. Growing up without a dad, you sort of filled that void for me. You are special to me, and I love you.

Mary Walts, Lowell, AR - 10/10/96

to – Roy

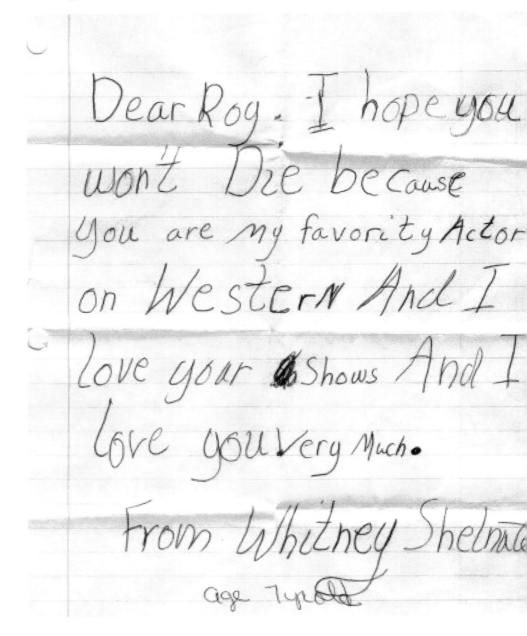

Dear Roy. I hope you won't Die because you are my favority Actor on Western And I love your Shows And I love you Very Much.

From Whitney Shelnutt age 7yr.

Whitney Shellnutt, Phil Campbell, AL - 9/30/96

to – Roy

I've been an ardent fan since I was 9 years old, and you have played a big part in my life without even knowing it. I am a woman of 60 now, but when I was young, my little girlfriend and I rode tree branch "horses," and I can just see myself now—long orange-red hair flying behind me like a horse's mane. One day I went to a movie, and there as big as life was the most handsome man I had ever seen in my young life. You! Dale, if you are reading this, you already know how many women love Roy, and a young girl's heart is pure, or at least it was back in those days. Anyway, I would not tell my friend that you played as "Roy Reynolds" because *her* last name was Reynolds and I was afraid she would get big-headed about it once she saw you. I bragged and bragged about you and told her she could keep pretending Gene Autry was her boyfriend, but that Roy Rogers was mine! I took her to your next movie with me and she fell as hard as I knew she would. In 1950 I married Warren Reynolds, my friend's uncle, and in 1955 we had a son, "Roy." I had forgotten about the Reynolds part in your movies and had named him "Roy" just for you. About 3 years ago my son bought me a "Roy" movie because he knew how much I liked them. When we watched, there it was! *You* playing the name of my son—Roy Reynolds! Until that moment I had forgotten about that portrayal. I never got to realize my dream of meeting you, but we go for drives quite a bit and pass through your boyhood home, frequently. Thank you for my wonderful childhood. I hope you stay around forever! PS. My son's middle name is Dale! *Ida Reynolds, Ashland, KY - 11/7/90*

1988 - Roy Dale Reynolds   1989 – Warren and Ida Reynolds enjoying Dollywood
- photos provided by Ida Reynolds

69

to – Roy

THEN (11/5/90): We enjoyed seeing you on the Country Music Awards and on the Randy Travis "Happy Trails" special. You looked great! We all love you and Dale and pray that you have many more happy years together. If you have seen any TV recently, you know there is a lot of trash on. We've been turning off the TV completely most nights unless there is a good show on Public Television. We have a few of your movies on tapes, so we enjoy those. John (5) and Sarah (2 ½) just love them. Sarah wants to wear her hair in a ponytail like Trigger! She also wants a horse like Trigger. "Entertainment Tonight" said your TV show would be put out on tape, and we are really looking forward to that! We love you!

Anne Marie, Mike, Michael, Jr., Matthew, Mark, John and Sarah Ann Clements

NOW (7/20/11): I now have many Roy and Dale movies, and I made a scrapbook of their lives. Everyone knows how much I love them both, and I talk about them all the time. I wear uniform tops at work with Roy and Dale on them, and I got to see Dusty last year! So exciting!"

Anne Marie Clements, Bangor, WI

Roy "Dusty" Rogers, Jr. and Anne Marie Clements
wearing her Roy Rogers work togs
– photo provided by Anne Marie Clements

to – Dale

We just today received a note from your personal secretary in answer to our letter and our snapshot autographed by Roy. He was so gracious, and what a thrill it was to be able to attend your church on Sunday morning during our trip to California. This note was indeed a joy to receive. Thank you both so much! It will have a very special place in our home.
John and Emilie Lenth, Garnavillo, IA - 5/16/92

to – Dale

I praise God for you and Roy. I remember those days when you were on the radio around suppertime. Mom would let me take my plate over near the radio and listen to the Roy Rogers show. That was my delight. Then in the early 1950s TV came into our house, and again I glued myself to my favorite show with Roy Rogers, Dale Evans, Trigger and Buttermilk. Then you started doing your own commercials with your adopted children, and I got to know some of their names. One of them was near my age, and I was so proud of being close in age to one of your adopted children. As the years went by, I thought how I wanted to pattern my life after you and Roy. This was before I knew about your littlest angel, Robin. At that time I didn't realize how much the words you wrote would change my life.

I got married and began having children. My oldest daughter was more like her father in her younger years—a little daring and challenging. She has now grown into a beautiful born-again young woman and given me 2 beautiful grandchildren, Renee Nicole and Scott Robert. And I praise God for that. Then came our own littlest "Angel Unaware." That's right, God gave us the most precious angel anyone could have. I'm not saying that it wasn't hard when I heard the first words out of the doctor's mouth, saying, "I don't know how to put it, but you have a very severely disabled child." Those words were a sharp-edged sword piercing my heart. Part of me wanted to run. Part of me became bitter and angry wanting to know why God had given me a child like this. And the rest of me sat in disbelief. I couldn't believe this was happening to me. What was I going to do? People looked down on those types of people and their families. What was I to do? I felt alone and abandoned, that is until God brought a special woman who had a special child like mine into my life. I had many decisions to make, and many I didn't want to make. Yet, sometimes we have no choice but to face things.

Well, I placed our littlest angel in a special home for children like him. It was only a two-week trial, and I spent more time there than at home. My heart was not in abandoning him, but instead in continuing to love him and care for him as I had been doing. This woman God had brought into my life held me tight and said, "I'm going to give you a book to read before you make any decisions. I know you are a Christian, and I know God will direct you in the right decisions." The book she handed me was *Angel Unaware*, written by you. I read it. It was *me* I was reading about. Your words told of what I was facing with our son. After this I was given another book to read, also written by you. It was toward the back of the book that God, through your words, helped me to make my decisions. I don't remember the words you said exactly, or the way you wrote them, as it's been so many years ago, yet I remember what you meant by those words—that you wouldn't, and neither would God, condemn anyone who had to place their children in a place where others could better care for them. You said we shouldn't feel guilty for doing so.

At that moment, I put the book down, got on my knees and prayed. I cried out loud to the Lord. Many tears filled my eyes, and my words are still as clear to me today as they were that day…"Lord, I have big decisions to make. If I am to put him away, I need a sign from you. If I am to keep him home, you will have to help me. I need all the strength and help you can give me. I can't do it alone. I'm scared, and I need an answer now, not tomorrow, not next week, but now." I was crying hard as I yelled out to my Father in prayer. I said, "If you really love like you say you do, you will give me my answer now." As my eyes slowly dried and focused, I realized that before me laid my Bible— open. Yes! Opened not closed. As I looked down, one of the scriptures on that page seemed to jump out at me, and a small, kind, loving voice spoke to me as I read this verse: *"Whatever decisions you make, I will be with you."* At that moment, I knew God had given me the answer I needed.

I brought our son home, and he will never leave my side until the Father takes him or I home. What a relief I felt. The first few years of his life, my son came close to death several times. As he grows older, the challenges are still there, only in a much different way. Now I see him growing into a young man of 28, yet mentally a child of between 6 months and 2 years. He might be a challenge, and we might have to give up a lot, but to see the love, strength, joy and peace in the eyes of our littlest angel is worth every bit of it. If I had to do it all over again, I would make the same decisions, for through our angel's life, I have grown in trust, faith, love, joy, peace and more. Our son isn't just touching our lives as a family, but many lives everywhere we go.

I mentioned early how much I wanted to be like you and Roy, to give something to those who had nothing, well, when our son became 2 years of age, we decided to make our lives even more challenging. We took in foster children, and shared the Lord with them. One day, we were asked if we could take another special angel from Heaven to love and care for. Well, you can probably guess the answer we gave. We grew close to this child, and every day we had him, he would show us a different picture in the Bible. Dale, I want you to know how much you and Roy have blessed me in so many different ways and how your books helped me in caring for our own littlest angel. I was only 7 when I first loved you, but now I am young at 56. Thanks for being my inspiration all these years.

Lucy Emsley, Puyallup, WA - 2/20/99

Essay

Here's the story of Roy's first wild turkey.

Roy came to Nebraska to go turkey hunting near Crawford and Fort Robinson on opening day. Robert B. Stringfellow, author of the 1950 book, *The Standard Guide to Hunting and Shooting*, accompanied him, along with former governor Robert Crosby; my father Willard Barbee, who was director of the Game Commission; two game officers; and Terry Carpenter, a Unicameral senator. They met at the fort the day before the season and headed out to the buttes to camp out. That night, sitting around the campfire, having a little libation, they began to sing cowboy songs—perfectly natural in the western setting they were in.

Then Roy decided he would see if his fellow hunters could follow along with a yodel he did. My dad could, but the others just began howling. They made so much noise that the coyotes began to howl with them. About half the night, Roy and Dad kept the coyotes answering.

Next day there was not a turkey to be found. No wonder since the birds probably thought they were in the middle of a food chain. That night, the hunters sat around the fire very quietly, hoping their prey would come back. They did, and Roy got his big turkey. My dad had been responsible for bringing the wild birds back to Nebraska three years before, and this was the first season. Roy may well have gotten the very first bird.

So that's the story of Roy's first wild turkey.

Kent Barbee - 10/12/03

The actual book given to Roy by the author during the turkey-hunting trip.

to – Roy

When I was a little girl my Dad and I used to watch your show together. He was a "hands on" dad. He had a cowboy hat, and I had my Dale Evans outfit. We would play "Roy and Dale" all the time. He would send notes to me and sign them from you. I was a very lucky little girl to have two wonderful men to look up to as I was growing up, you and my great Dad. My dad died almost eleven years ago. I miss him deeply. At his funeral, I passed his casket, placed my hand on it and whispered, "Happy Trails." Something just between the two of us, but that's how deeply our time with you meant to us. Thank you for the most wonderful memories I had with my dad.

Anne Saracino, Rye, NY - 11/6/90

---

to – Roy

As a boy growing up during the 50s we had Sugar Pops and Roy Rogers every Saturday morning. Who needed more? I want to thank you for the inspiration and solid role model that you were to me in my life as I grew up.

Greg Schrader, New Carlsbad, IN - 10/2/96

Roy Rogers and Sugar Pops® fan Greg Schrader
- photo provided by Greg Schrader

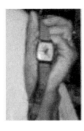

to – Roy

THEN (11/17/90): As a 47-year-old lady, you are still my hero. Recently I found someone who could repair my childhood "Roy Rogers" watch, and I wear it so proudly.

Margaret Anne Orr, Corinth, MS

NOW (7/6/11):
Margaret Anne Orr and her Roy Rogers watch still going strong.

Margaret Anne Orr
– photo provided by Margaret Anne Orr

to – Roy and Dale

In our minds you both shine the brightest of all movie stars. The love and the kindness you both gave so openly to us all is what we remember most. We will never forget it.

Jim and Abby Kern, Catawissa, MO - 11/7/90

to – Roy

I had the pleasure of meeting you and co-interviewing you in 1975 when you visited the Morning Show on WBT in Charlotte, North Carolina. You were there to promote your movie "McIntosh and T.J."

I found you to be just what I had hoped you would be—a warm, friendly person much like the Roy Rogers on the screen. I told you that your good examples helped me when I was a kid. I grew up trying to be like Roy Rogers.

I pray that you will soon be back on your feet and feeling great again. Millions love you, Roy, and we want to see you up and around. I really enjoyed the recent "Happy Trails" special on TNN with you and Randy Travis.

Here's some trivia for you. I was a deejay on the midnight shift at WBT, and in 1978, Lib Hatcher of Country Palace called to ask if she could bring Moe Bandy by for an interview. I said, "of course." Along with Lib and Moe was a young 18-year-old boy, Randy Traywick. Lib said she hoped to record Randy soon and would let me be the first to play his record.

Well, in July, she came back with a record called "Dreamin'," which I thought was good. I told Randy that he had a great voice but needed to get a better band to back him up next time. So I guess I was the first deejay to play a Randy Travis record 12 years ago. I met Roy Rogers and Randy Travis at WBT. Lucky me! Next time you see Randy ask him about that record, "Dreamin'." The song never did make it, but it was a good start for him.

I will watch for you soon on TNN, Roy. Take care. Tell Dale how much she has meant to us also. I collect cowboy movies—Roy Rogers, Rocky Lane, Charles Starrett, Wild Bill Elliott, etc. I remember one of my questions to you when I helped interview you at WBT. "What kind of person was Roy Barcroft? You said he was a fine man. I was glad to hear it because I thought he did a great job also.

God bless you, Roy, for all you've meant to all of us. I treasure the photo you autographed for me in 1975. With my best personal regards,

Larry James, Decatur, AL – 11/8/90 - Radio Personality and 1978 CMA (Country Music Association) award winner for Medium Market On-Air Personality of the Year

to – Roy

I was a part of the Montana Cattle drive last July. It was such a thrill to meet my lifetime hero and your lovely "bride." I'm enclosing a copy of the picture that I dreamed of all my life—meeting you. This picture is our Christmas card this year! God bless you and Dale with many Happy Trails. *Helen Twedt, Rudyard, MT - 11/19/90*

Roy Rogers, a very happy Helen Twedt, and Randy Travis
- photo provided by Helen Twedt

Added by Helen's daughter, Deb Schmidt, on 10/9/11:

We lost my mom in 2001. We surely miss her but are so happy that she got to meet Roy in her lifetime. She was so ecstatic. There's a funny story about that July 1990 day...

My dad did not accompany my mom to the cattle drive because he was involved in a four-wheeler accident the night before they were to leave. Mom rushed him to the hospital where they learned he crushed a disc in his back. He was hospitalized, but Mom didn't want to miss the one chance she would ever have to meet Roy, so she went with a friend and left Dad in the hospital. We all thought it was very funny, especially my dad. But he didn't want her to miss her chance to be with her hero either. He was happy she went because he knew how happy it would make her.

The following is from my mom's diary of the day:

My friend, Grace, and I left at 7 am for Columbus, Montana, and checked into a motel upon arrival. The next morning we drove about 28 miles of curvy roads to Roscoe, Montana—so excited! We were picked up and shuttled to the cattle drive site that evening. We were allowed to do anything we wished, so we walked all over then went through the food line for a steak supper. For the next four hours we watched the Nashville Network film at the campfire. It was fantastic to watch and MEET my hero, Roy. I was in a state of total awe! I also met Randy Travis, Denver Pyle, and Dale Evans, but my eyes were on Roy. He told me he made his first movie in January 1938. The Nashville Network had a lot of retakes, but it was great. We lasted until 11:30 pm before being taken back to Roscoe. I was exhausted but so glad we had the chance to be there. I still can't believe that I actually met and saw Roy Rogers in person—a moment I've waited all my life to experience. To actually meet your hero? WOW! I pray the pictures turned out!

---

to – Roy

If there is a person in the world worth remembering with love and admiration, you are him. The glitter of your life will stay forever, like that of the diamond which brilliance remains till eternity. Remember me as your unseen friend.

your around-the-world fan from the Philippines - 1996

Essay

Roy Rogers means more to me than perhaps he does to most of his fans. He fulfilled my need for a male figure in my life because, as a youngster, he *was* the man in my life. He served as my father, my pastor, my hero...and my Bible.

My father was a hard drinking, swearing, carousing, and ne'er-do-well individual. We did not attend church, so what Christian principles I received were instilled in me by Roy and his films. It was Roy who totally influenced the good in me in my formative years. He taught me the Golden Rule and so much more. I contribute a lot of what I am today to the example set by Roy Rogers. I am active in my church, and I do not drink, smoke or swear. I am far from perfect, but I would be even further from perfect if Roy Rogers had not come into my life. Every boy needs a hero he can look up to. Roy was that man for me. Not only did his movies influence me, but more importantly, so did his personal life.

Roy's life personifies the Judeo-Christian values that made our country strong. Let me cite some examples.

1. He displayed total integrity, stood up for what is right, and his word was his bond. It is told that when he signed with Art Rush to be his manager, he never had a contract, only a handshake, and Rush was his manager until Rush died.

2. Roy's films delivered wholesome entertainment, and when Republic tried to force him to play a smart-alecky, smoking, drinking reporter in a movie, he refused and left the studio, telling them this was not the image that the public expected of Roy Rogers. He did not return until the studio relented and told him he did not have to do the movie.

3. He steadfastly refused to do ads for alcohol and tobacco. For a while Roy enjoyed a beer and a cigarette, but one day he said, "I thought to myself, what if a photographer took my picture drinking a beer and the kids saw it? I decided right then and there that that was not the

image that I wanted the kids to see, so I quit." Regarding smoking, he said, "They said it caused cancer, and I believe them."

4. Roy was a patriot and loved the U.S.A. During World War II, he made exhausting personal appearance tours to sell millions of dollars in War Bonds and cheer up our service men and women.

5. In most of his films Roy played himself, and it was easy to do because he was the same person off screen as he was in his films. Dale said, "There is no façade about Roy, what you see on screen is exactly like he is in real life."

6. Roy not only boldly proclaimed his Christianity, he took a stand when it was challenged. He always closed his performances with a hymn. When he was told at a Madison Square Garden rodeo that he could not do the hymn, he said to Dale, "Mama (he often called her Mama,) if we can't do the hymn, we'll just go home." This would have cost Roy a ton of money. When the rodeo officials saw that he meant what he said about not showing up, they knew it would cost them much of their audience and agreed that they could include the hymn.

7. Another time, a boy wrote Roy about his playmates making fun of him because he went to Sunday school. Roy answered in front of thousands of kids telling the boy that going to Sunday school was the right thing to do. Later he mailed out cards telling the kids the importance of going to Sunday school.

8. Roy was a loving husband and father, with numerous grandchildren and great-grandchildren. He and Dale had an international family, adopting Dodie, an American Indian girl, Debbie, a Korean girl, and Sandy, a boy who had been physically abused. Marion, a foster daughter from Scotland, came to live with them as a teenager. In addition, Roy and Dale devoted an enormous amount of time and money to children and children's charities, and they established the Happy Trails Children's Foundation to care for neglected or abused children. Roy made countless visits to hospitals and orphanages, and he was known to make phone calls to cheer up sick and dying children.

9. Roy was a man of strength who overcame tragedies that would have forever crippled a lesser man. He lost his wife, Arline only a few days after the birth of Dusty, which left him with an infant and two small girls, Cheryl and Linda. Later he and Dale lost three children— Debbie, their adopted Korean daughter who died in a church bus crash when she was twelve; Sandy, their adopted son who died while serving in the Army in Germany; and their only biological offspring, Robin, a Down's Syndrome child.

10. Roy was called "King of the Cowboys" but he never lost humility. He made friends and kept them, and he was well respected by those with whom he worked.

11. He was honored with practically every humanitarian award available, and he appreciated his fans. As long as he was able, he would go daily to his museum to greet, shake hands, and pose for photos with fans.

I know Roy wasn't perfect, but he was about as perfect as a human can be. He greatly influenced the lives of generations of youngsters, and I can think of no better example for children (or grownups for that matter.)

For all the things listed above, and many more, I am a fan of Roy's, and he has meant more to me through the years than I could ever express.

Bobby Copeland, author of 16 books on western stars, their horses, their loves and their lives -

Author Bobby Copeland with a selection of his western books

- photo provided by Bobby Copeland

to – Roy

THEN (10/31/90): I am a 46-year-old man and I don't often write fan letters. Growing up in the late 40s and early 50s was a terrific experience. You and Dale Evans were a large part of the reason that it was so terrific. The wholesome entertainment that you provided was not only fun, it taught many of the lessons that our generation considers to be of great value. Today's entertainment should get back to some of those basics and maybe our moral values would do the same. I only wish that my children and grandchildren could know and live in the world I grew up in. I'll get off my soapbox now and just wish you the best of health and family happiness. You are a blessed couple and an inspiration to millions.

NOW (7/11/11): I admired the way Roy and Dale chose to entertain all of us of that generation. I also admired the way they lived their lives, and the generosity of their spirits. They produced clean and wholesome entertainment for all of us and adhered to the belief that we are deeply affected by what we see and what we surround ourselves with. It was a simpler time and a gentler time for young people in this country. Roy and Dale's talent, their music and their ideals, were gifts that were shared with all of us who were fortunate enough to be present in their time. They were people of faith and shared their incredible lives with their children and lived what they represented.

Bill Paquette, Ballston Lake, NY

to – Dale

We wanted you to know that we are still thinking of you and praying for you. You are so loved and remembered. May you enjoy our daughter's poem.

Don, Edie, Jeanette, Alyssa and David Newton, Linn Grove, IN - 12/31/98

"**Where Happy Trails Shall Meet Again**" by Alyssa A. Newton

One night when the sunset tinted
The thrilling azure of the skies,
From Heaven's Pearly Gates there peered
Three bright-faced children's searching eyes.
Turning, down the streets one sprinted
Until God's tow'ring throne she neared.

With fervent, yet respectful tone,
As all so often she implored,
"O Father, when will they get here?"
Her voice inquired of the Lord.
"Your Father's work on earth is done:
His chosen time is drawing near."

Upon the child's sweet upturned face,
The Lord bestowed a loving smile,
"Now run and tell the stablemen,
'Go curry Trigger's coat awhile,
And put his saddle into place,
While rounding up the able men
To put Roy Rogers' ranch to rights."

The child clapped her hands in glee,
Then raced off to do as bidden.
"Sandy! Debbie! Listen to me!
Our Daddy's coming home tonight!"
Oh, their joy could not be hidden!

Young Robin was in giddy form,
And could not keep her body still;
Miss Debbie tidied up her hair
To satisfy her happy will;
While Sandy, in his uniform,
Assumed his stately soldier's air.

Then Trigger, with a wild whinny,
Full galloped down a golden street—
Nostrils flaring, mane all streaming,
He flew along on hooves more fleet
Than a mortal horse or any
Phantom one encounters dreaming.

Straight down a rainbow, through
the gates
Quite lightning-like, he clove the
skies
With such speed, he left them
burning—
As when a comet through them flies.

Upon the earth 'twas very late,
And, within his bed was turning
Trigger's rider, deeply sleeping,
Until, outside, Roy heard a snort—
A sound which snapped him to his
feet.
From bed to back the leap was
short—
As Roy's body still lay sleeping,
Off they galloped down the street!

Through the Gates, right from the
rainbow,
Trig with his rider road again,
Hooves sparking fire from golden
streets,
Until they reached God's throne.
And then,
The Cowboy's King with Trig did
bow,
As the King of Earth they did meet.

With O! what joy was Heaven filled,
As Roy arose from kneeling there,
For young Robin stood before him—
His tiny Angel Unaware.
And as the crowds around them
milled,
Some angels fleetly bore them

Around a curve in Heaven's streets.
And there Roy Rogers found his
home,
In Heaven's sleepy Western side,
Where many bygone fans had come
To help Roy Rogers' children greet
Their father, aft' his Homeward ride.

As Roy, on Trigger's brawny back,
Came trotting up the golden street,

Pat Brady opened wide the gate
Which led to pastures green and
sweet,
Where Heaven's horses never
lacked—
No matter how much Trigger ate!
Then Sandy snapped a smart
salute,
As Debbie combed her Daddy's hair,
And Robin gaily frisked about,
Beneath old Bullet's watchful care.
Then standing in his cowboy boots,
Roy with his family set out

To look up Gabby Hayes and all
The singing Sons of Pioneers,
As well as all Roy's loyal fans
Who welcomed him with hearty
cheers.
And always, within easy call,
Grazed Trigger, near the joyful
bands.

On earth, next day, when all awoke
And found that Roy had ridd'n away
To heavenly pastures in the sky,
All those on earth had good to say
About Roy Rogers when they spoke,
In voices laden with sad sighs.

But could they see how Roy is now,
With Trig and Bullet by his side,
They would possess no drear regrets
That Roy chose to Homeward ride—
For there no worry twists his brow,
Nor is his face all traced with sweat.

For thus end all Happy Trails
Of those who take Christ as their
Guide:
Christ said to Roy, *"Let's ride my
friend,"*
And Roy just saddled up to ride,
Knowing he'd be, when daylight
failed,
Where Happy Trails shall meet
again.

Alyssa A. Newton, Age 17 - August of 1998

to – Dale

Roy did so much for me in my formative years, showing a rather nondescript teenager that there was a real world out there in which it was possible to find real friendship and a joy in living. I enjoyed all the films, particularly those in which you both appeared, sometimes in the early days of "continuous" showings, sitting through them two or three times. I often tried to figure out what it was that held such a special magic for me, and came to the conclusion that Roy, Bob Nolan and the Sons of the Pioneers, Gabby Hayes, and of course, Dale Evans, were really friends off screen as well as on, and it was this aura which seemed to translate onto the movie screen, taking me into that magic world with you all. I am not far behind Roy in years, being 70 now, and I still enjoy many of my old favorites on video, like "Lights of Old Santa Fe." One song you sang as a duet with Roy in that movie is still firmly etched in my memory…*"When the breeze blows the leaves around, and the trees make a gentle sound, from the hills I can see them shining, see the lights of Old Santa Fe."* I can still remember hearing those words then the culture shock of walking out of the movie house into the cold, damp reality of an English winter! So thanks, Dale, to both you and Roy, for although I never met you, you made my world a brighter and happier place. By offering friendship, which was one of Roy's great attributes, I have built a circle of friends among British, American, Canadian, and now Australian, people. I guess I will be a fan and an admirer of you both for as long as I'm around.

Trevor (T. T.) Mullins, Seaford, South Australia - 10/23/98

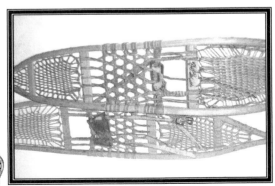

to – Roy

We are Brazilian and we love you since our childhood. May God bless you forever.

Norton and Cassia Coll, Sao Paulo, Brazil - 1/1/91

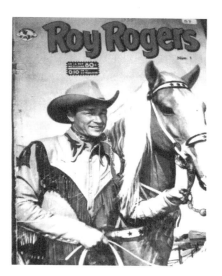 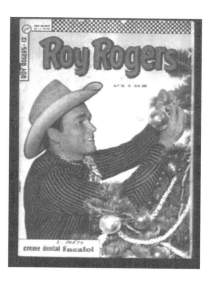

Four Vintage Brazilian Roy Rogers Comics provided by Norton and Cassia Coll

to – Roy & Dale

I'm sure you have heard many times how much you mean to people, and since this is true in my life, I am going to tell you again. Roy and Dale, you have set such a wonderful example of what married life and family should be like. The closeness, the love that comes from within you, shines to the whole world. When I see you on TV, I feel your message of love in my life. We have a very close and loving relationship with our two sons. I really believe this is all due in part to the influence you have had on my life. I have read all of Dale's books, cried and wondered how you could survive such heartaches. But I know it has to be your faith in God and your love for family. You see, I only had two brothers – one died when he was 9 months old from pneumonia, and the other was killed in a head-on-collision by a man who said he could have avoided hitting him. I will never get over my loss, but I see you pick up the pieces and go on, so I can go on, too. I have never written a fan letter to anyone before. I have told my husband many times that of all the people in the world, I would most love to see you in person. I am honest and totally believe in giving "roses while you live." Roy and Dale, you deserve a huge bouquet. You are wonderful, the greatest – my heroes.

Karen Vandevender, Bergoo, WV - 1/9/91

to – Roy and Dale

I am 55 years old and remember you with such fondness for all the many years of western movies and songs. I have a few movies on my VCR here at home of you. We all love you. My parents knew Gabby Hayes long ago. God bless you both.

Mike Shabala III, Rochester, NY -9/28/96

Essay

I have been blessed with two lovely daughters and four grandkids—one girl and three boys. I became a fan of Roy Rogers even before his first wife passed. My dad, who was a police officer at the time, would bring the ten-cent Roy Rogers comics home to me, especially when I was sick. He would come home at lunch with a book under his arm and come into my room and read the book to me.

When Roy and Dale's TV show started I would watch it each time it was on. Their clean living was one of the things they would try and teach the kids. I also remember how upset I was when Roy married Dale. I would tell my parents that I wanted to grow up to marry him, so why couldn't he wait?

I think I've bought most of the books Dale has written, and best of all I still have around 50 comic books. Some are not in really good shape due to the boys on my street that used to exchange comics. They would always try to cheat me out of the 25-cent ones. They always said they should get four ten-cent comics for a quarter. So of course a heated debate would get started with one while another one would sneak comics out of my box.

One year Roy and Dale brought their rodeo to San Antonio. We had first-row seats, and after their show I went around to the back entrance and tried to give Roy a picture of him that I had drawn, but alas, I couldn't get it to him.

On Saturday mornings I would walk about two miles to the movies to see at least five cartoons, one serial and a full-length feature. Twenty-five cents paid for the movie, candy, popcorn and a drink. The best times I had was when the movie was with Roy Rogers.

Then in 1968 Roy and Dale's show came to our arena. My dad was the greatest. He made sure that my husband and I got a front-row seat. And to make the evening even better, he got me a backstage pass. Some nice man took me to the dressing rooms. I waved at Pat Brady. Dale was not ready, so I missed her, but then the man knocked on a door, and Roy answered. I shook his hand...I think. The man told Roy I was a fan, and Roy said, "Thank you. I hope you enjoy the show." What I remember is that my voice cracked as I tried to say so many, many things to him about how much I enjoyed his movies, how much I loved the way he raised his kids and lived his life, but I think all that came out was "----------------." Nothing. Nothing at all would come out. My voice must have stayed home. I went back out and watched the show. When Roy was not on stage he sat down right in front of us, about ten feet away. I took pictures of him there.

I always wanted a horse like Trigger. Never did get the horse, but I have a home-based craft business and its name is Golden Cloud Designs. In case you're going "huh?" it's because Trigger's name was Golden Cloud when Roy bought him. Roy changed it to Trigger. Also the first car I learned to drive in was a jeep, like Nellybelle.

For over fifty years I never missed but three of our once-a-year rodeos. My mom made me a western shirt with embroidered designs on it, something like Roy would have worn.

I only wish that I could have gone to Apple Valley while Roy and Dale were there to try and meet them again. Maybe then I would have been able to talk, with sound that is, something that could actually be heard.

Roy and Dale influenced my life by just seeing them and hearing about all of their blessings and all of their hard times, and how they overcame them. I know that my faith in God is not anywhere close to theirs, but I do believe in God. I've had hard times and still have a few, but when I think about how I should handle something, I think back to how Roy and Dale would handle it. Like them, I give my heart and my problems to God, for I know that he will help me through everything.

I think the world could use a lot more Roys and Dales in our lives. Every time I think about them being gone, I tear up, and knowing that Roy Jr. had to sell everything makes me so very sad. I only wish that I was rich and could buy everything, but I'm not. I've been disabled with Parkinsons since '96, but I've found that saying it out loud makes it a little easier to handle. I have Roy and Dale to thank for that honesty.

Pat Banks, San Antonio, TX - 11/4/03

1968 – Roy Rogers resting off-stage

1968 – Roy Rogers and Dale Evans leaving

1968 - Roy Rogers - Texas performance
- 3 photos provided by Pat Banks

---

to – Roy

My great American heroes:

Abraham Lincoln
Ronald Reagan
Will Rogers
John Wayne
Roy Rogers and Dale Evans

We love you all so much for all you've done and for the many years of great entertainment you've given so many. We need you, Roy. We do.

Connie, Delbert and Kami Stebens, Liberal, KS - 10/9/96

---

to – Roy & Dale

I'm really not too good at words, but I want you to know that you have given us a lot of entertainment and love with your shows. You made it a Heaven down here on earth for a lot of fans, especially me. I have seen all your movies and I also have a collection of your films on tape. I watch you every chance I get when you make appearances on TV. Your new tape with Clint Black is also exceptional. I also have your tapes with Dale and Dusty. I have been your #1 fan for over fifty years, and I will always be that fan. You are an inspiration to us all.

Donna Lonergan, Niagra Falls, Ontario, Canada - 10/1/96

to – Dale & Family

We all loved your dad, husband and grandpa. Roy was the finest role model for everyone. We love you all so much.

Ron, Sonia, Julie, Ronnie, David and Jonathan Brown, Clewiston, FL - 10/14/98

The Ron Brown Family – photo provided by Ron Brown

It was great getting to work with my hero, the guy I grew up watching on the big screen. He was everything that I thought he was and more! We became good friends, and you can't ask for anything better than that.

Dean Smith, Olympic Gold Medallist, Rodeo Champion, Hollywood Stuntman

Dean Smith and Trigger, doubling for Roy Rogers
on the TV show, "The Fall Guy"
- photo provided by Dean Smith

93

to – Roy

You don't know me, but I have been a big fan of yours since the 1950s when I was a young girl. I thought you were the sexiest cowboy on TV. I loved your show on Saturday mornings, and there were many times I would feign illness from Catechism so I could stay home and watch you, Dale, Trigger and the rest of the crew.

Denise Pekarek's Roy Rogers desk collage
– photo provided by Denise Pekarek

Life was much simpler back then and we were happy to own a black and white television. Something we have in common is that we share the same birth date, November 5th. I am celebrating a half a century this year, but I sure feel good! I want to wish you "Happy Birthday" and hope you have a great day. It's nice to share a birthday with someone who is your hero and someone you admire. I have to tell you a little story about a trip I took with a couple of friends a few years ago. I have the "Roy Rogers Tribute" CD where you sing with the country/western singers, and I just love it. I taped it so I could take it on the trip. Needless to say, I practiced my yodeling, much to the dismay of my friends! And "Tumbling Tumbleweeds" became our theme song as we cruised through the prairies of Nebraska, Wyoming, Colorado and South Dakota. We had a great trip! I am still angry with my husband and son-in-law for not stopping in Victorville during a trip we once made from San Diego to Las Vegas. They thought I was joking when I told them I wanted to stop, and it was several miles down the road when I finally convinced them that I was serious. But it was too late! They still hear about it. The picture is of a little collage I have at my desk. "Happy Trails" is my theme song! Thanks for providing me with so very much!

Denise Pekarek, Fridley, MN - 10/15/96

to – Roy

I've never written a fan letter in my life, but I've been meaning to write to you for many years to tell you that I've adored you since I was six years old. That's 53 years! You were a good influence on kids, and they sure need someone like you today. I had a baby brother when I was seven, and my parents named him Roger because of my love for you. Plus, my son was born in 1958, and his name is Leonard. I know that is your real name. How about that? Anyway, you've been a huge part of my life and still are. I went to see you at Soldier Field in the late 40s. It rained, and you ended up just going from one car to another. I sat and cried while my Dad cussed. But I still loved you. Still do!!

Janet Pennada, Streamwood, IL - 10/1/96

---

to – Roy

From the early days
On black and white TV
You were always there for me.

Catching the bad guys
Singing songs
Teaching everyone right from wrong.

The Good Guy always
Kisses his horse
But never the leading lady, of course!

Roy, you, Dale and Trigger
You see
Have given so many great memories.

So keep up the good work,
And get well real quick
Sincerely, Diane Perry, an old sidekick."

Diane Perry, Palmdale, CA
11/13/90

to – Roy

You are a friend, as I have "known" you for many years. This world NEEDS you! We (millions of us) need you and what you stand for – decency, family, goodness and everything beautiful. I have had 4 lifetimes in one, so it seems. So much of my life could not be described as only a nightmare because it's been H_ _ L. There's just no other word for it. But life is hope and there is always a chance for something better. Several years ago I told someone close to me that if one more bad thing happens, I will give up. I've cried, prayed, and kept on trying. Recession took our jobs, house, car and furniture. We both have health problems, and my husband is handicapped. But I have your movies on tape and your pictures in scrapbooks, and with misty eyes I say, "you give me strength." You are a constant love in my world. You can't know how grateful I am for that.

A fan, Chicago, IL - 9/30/96

to – Roy

When I was young I had a king size crush on you. And my current gentleman friend had a similar crush on your lovely wife, Dale Evans (and still does!) We are both always rooting for you!

Helen Sayatovic, Euclid, OH - 11/13/90

1950 - Sherry and Sandy Hoover in their Dale Evans cowgirl outfits with Roy Rogers
-photo provided by Mrs. James Hoover

to – Roy

I would just like to say thank you for your many years of being role models to young people. We met you when you came to Birmingham, Alabama in 1950. Lou Weiner conducted a contest to find a young person to appear with you at our auditorium. My daughters Sherry and Sandy were 3 and 5 at the time and were chosen. They sang "I Didn't Know the Gun Was Loaded." Sherry and Sandy are now 51 and 49 and have grown children of their own, but they have never forgotten the thrill of meeting you both. In everyone's heart you are still the King of the Cowboys, and you are just as popular today as you were when you first started. You have enriched lives!

Mrs. James Hoover, Birmingham, AL - 10/1/96

to – Roy

THEN (11/12/90): Though we've never met, you've played a very important part in my life—my first hero. In fact, I remember naming my first bicycle, Trigger. I was born in western Pennsylvania, and the severe winters forced my brother, sister and me to play indoors most of the time. We spent countless hours playing in our full basement. My sister was Dale Evans, my brother was Bullet, and I was always Roy Rogers. There are photographs of me sporting my cowgirl duds, but I was always Roy Rogers in my heart! We moved to Texas when I was only five. Imagine my disappointment when I discovered that Texas was not really where you lived! Today I'm a 42-year-old schoolteacher. You instilled many of the values I've carried with me through the years. You taught some pretty strong lessons in your movies and TV series. Over the years you've seen misfortune and lost loved ones, but your faith never seemed to waiver. You count your blessings and not your woes. We all need to remember to do that. Someone once asked me what famous person I'd most want to meet. It didn't take long for me to come up with my answer—Roy Rogers! I've taught third grade for the past seventeen years. Working with young children, I've discovered they have no heroes to look up to today. As you once shared in a song, I had Hoppy, Gene, and most importantly, you! For this I will be forever grateful. Happy Trails with love!

NOW (6/21/11): **"Happy Trails"** by Trudy Taylor

Dale and Roy brought so much joy
To the children of my day.

Roy stressed what was good and right
And never fought an unfair fight.
I never once heard him cuss...
He expected nothing less of us.

Dale, his faithful partner,
Was always at his side.
She followed him to Heaven
Soon after he had died.

Growing up, my stick horse
Didn't have a name.
When I got a little bigger,
My trusty bike was "Trigger."

Though they're gone, they're not forgotten
Roy would soon turn 100,
But he's in my heart and in my mind.
He left lots of "kids" who still love him behind.

Rest in peace, Roy and Dale, your lessons have served us well.
It still brings a tear to my eye to hear someone sing..."Happy Trails"

Trudy Taylor, Pollok, TX

1990 - Fat Boys – photo provided by Damon Wimbley

to – Roy

We've come to know over the years when we are on tour and riding along in our bus, we can't wait to stop to get some Roy Rogers good chicken. Get back in the saddle, Roy. We love you, Roy.

The Fat Boys - 11/9/90

to – Dale

I am not accustomed to writing famous people or strangers, but this is one time that is very important that I do write. One reason is that when I was a small child, the movies that you and your husband made were among the very few rays of hope I had of a life that might be decent and normal. Somehow, even though it was only a movie, your decency and sincerity still came through as real. The second reason I want to write is to tell you that I work with about 50 people, and during the course of time I have known them, we've sat in our break room at work and watched the news on TV many times. I have been in that break room on many occasions when announcements were made about the passing of different famous people. Never did I see the sadness so apparent as I did when the news covered Roy's death. It so touched me to see that all those people felt the same as I did. The two of you held up decency and family all of these years, whether it helped your careers or hindered them. That is not done very often in show business. I want also to tell you that I hope that when some time passes, you will consider writing another book. You've never been as wise and experienced as you are today. Situations that you have coped with may seem mundane to you, but I, and others, would love to know about them. I want to thank you from my heart for all the enjoyment that you gave me as a child and for the example you set for family life. You have always shown grace and generosity.

Modell Fleenor, Gahanna, OH - 9/30/98

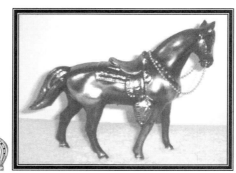

Essay

When Roy and Dale's museum closed, many feared the public would no longer get to enjoy the fruits of their wonderful life. But people are sharing their newfound treasures in a public way, some through adding to their exhibits and others by sharing personal remembrances. Shared memories foster the making of new friends with those we may never have otherwise known.

I am dedicated to preserving western heritage and to keeping my family's memories alive by enlightening and sharing their legacy and introducing them to younger generations whose only knowledge of what they represent comes from the stories they are told. Roy was without question the King of the Cowboys, and I'm proud to share a few of the memories of three men who were not only friends of Roy and Dale, but singing cowboys themselves—my grandfather, Taylor Curtis "Cactus Mack" McPeters, and his two cousins, Glenn Strange and Rex Allen. All were close personal friends of Roy & Dale, and I was lucky to grow up with these great men, hearing their amazing stories.

One fun tale is how Roy Rogers once came to be known as Cactus Mack. Roy was a part of one of my grandfather's earliest bands: *Cactus Mack and his O Bar O Cowboys.* Roy, known then by his birth name Leonard Slye (Len to his friends) joined the band at an early point in his musical career. The band, named after an old Arizona brand, was the first professional musical affiliation the two musicians shared together. Other band mates were "Slumber" Nichols, "Cyclone" the fiddle player, and the late, great, Tim Spencer.

Together the men set off on what their booking agent heralded as a "barnstorming trip through the Southwest." He assured success, stating unequivocally that "Those folks will appreciate fine Western Music." The problem was, he only "loosely" arranged their gigs, and in addition to scheduling delays, they nearly starved to death from lack of funds. It was, in Roy's words *"the most unsuccessful tour of its kind in history."* Upon their return to Cactus Mack's hometown of Willcox, Arizona, a banner over Main

Street greeted them. *"Hometown Boy Makes Good! Welcome, Cactus Mack and Friends"* it said. That warm welcome felt like a soothing balm, and after such a miserable run, Cactus decided to leave the band and stay home. Len was able to talk the others into going on to Roswell, New Mexico for the second leg of the tour. Wishing to hold onto the notoriety Cactus had achieved as a musician, Len opted to retain the moniker of the band, still billing them as *'Cactus Mack and his O Bar O Cowboys'* even though there was no Cactus!

Roy later told my grandfather a funny story about the repercussions of his decision. It seems that Cactus Mack had a follower in Roswell who decided to drop in and see him while they were there, only it wasn't Cactus Mack who answered the door. It was Roy. And when the follower asked for Cactus Mack, and Roy professed to be him, the big guy didn't miss a beat. He just eyed Roy up and down and pronounced that ole Cactus Mack sure had changed a lot since the last time they'd laid eyes on each other. Sheepishly, Roy had no choice but to confess that he'd sort of temporarily "adopted" my grandfather's identity.

Unfortunately, the trip's second leg was awful, and at one point Roy borrowed a rifle from a radio station manager and went hunting just to find food to survive. The men would remember that gnawing hunger all their lives.

The silver lining to this story is that it was in Roswell where Len met Arline Wilkins who, in 1936, would become his second wife. Roy had commented on a radio show just how much he missed his mom's lemon pies. Arline called in and promised him a whole lemon pie if he'd do "The Swiss Yodel" during the next day's show. He studied all night, performed the song, and received his luscious lemon reward. A dinner invitation followed, and later, marriage. My grandmother, Cactus' wife Etta, thought a lot of Arline, and in those early days they were friends.

This early trail leads to the well-known conclusion where Leonard Slye becomes Roy Rogers and finds huge success with the *Sons of the Pioneers.* As for Cactus Mack, after some basking in the warmth of family, his desire to move to Hollywood became impossible to ignore. Both he and his cousin Glenn Strange (best known as 'Sam' the bartender in *Gunsmoke,*) headed west, and in 1933, threw in with the Hoot Gibson Rodeo where Cactus became their announcer. Cactus was a rolling stone with a fascinating career, and he and Roy's paths would continue to cross until Cactus' sudden death in 1962.

Cactus and Glenn were wonderful singer/songwriters, often writing the scores for movies they appeared in. They played alongside film greats Buck Jones, Tom Tyler, Tim McCoy, Johnny Mack Brown, John Wayne and Tex Ritter in the years before making movies with Roy. Cactus & Roy's first movie together was the 1939 movie *Frontier Pony Express. Days of Jesse James, Sheriff of Tombstone,* and *Bells of Rosarita* followed before they moved on to TV, where Cactus, usually playing a bad guy, frequently appeared in *The Roy Rogers Show* during its six-year run on ABC. In one episode, Cactus was supposed to kidnap and kill Trigger. Luckily Roy rode to Trigger's rescue. Good thing...that's something no one wants to be remembered for!

Roy was also close friends with Rex Allen, the Arizona Cowboy, who was another cousin to my Grandfather Cactus and Glenn Strange. Roy and Rex had much in common, including their passion for the glitzy, fringed clothing made by Nudie, the Rodeo Tailor. Nudie and Roy remained friends for all their lives, and there were sure some great parties with legendary guests such as Sunset Carson, Tex Williams, Monte Hale, Denver Pyle, and Rex and Roy. One personal Rex and Roy story tells the tale of how it was that Rex teamed up with his beloved horse KoKo, "The Miracle Horse of the Movies."

Koko, a chocolate Morgan with a light mane and tail, was ten years old when Rex "found" him in the possession of his good friend, Roy Rogers. As the story goes, Roy initially bought the horse for his wife, but at that time, Dale was not the great rider she eventually became, and Roy feared she wasn't ready for such a lively mount. Roy discussed this problem with Rex, and Rex suggested he take a look at the horse. It was love at first sight. Roy was also to have exclaimed to Rex that not only was 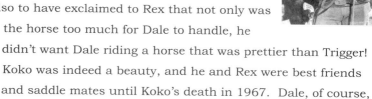 the horse too much for Dale to handle, he didn't want Dale riding a horse that was prettier than Trigger! Koko was indeed a beauty, and he and Rex were best friends and saddle mates until Koko's death in 1967. Dale, of course,

rode into the sunset each week on a light buckskin Quarter Horse, Buttermilk, who appeared with her in numerous Westerns until his death in 1972.

Earlier, I spoke of Nudie's friendship with my family, and handed down through the generations, that friendship remains intact today between Nudie's granddaughter, Jamie, and myself. Nudie once gifted Roy with one of his fabulously festooned Cadillacs, complete with a covered wagon trailer to pull behind it. Both were on display at the Roy and Dale museum in Apple Valley until it closed its doors. Jamie and I recently traveled together to the Christies "Roy Rogers" auction in New York in the hopes of winning back the little trailer. We were blessed with the good fortune of the winning bid, then challenged by the misfortune of me being misquoted by the press. Gee, imagine that! But the important part is that Nudie's gift to Roy is back in the family where it belongs. We've always had a great relationship with the Rogers family, and they couldn't have been happier to see that little 'memory' make the full circle back to the Nudie family, knowing it would continue to be shared with the public.

Memories are wonderful things. The threads of history are woven tightly, the skein of events up for interpretation. I hope the legacies of Roy and Dale, and the impact they've made on this country, move into the tapestry of the lives of generations to come. Happy Trails Roy and Dale! We miss you...

Julie Ann Ream, 2007 recipient of the "Cowboy Keeper Award" presented by the National Day of the Cowboy for her work in preserving America's Western Heritage and Cowboy Culture, producer of the *Western Legends Awards*, contributor to the annual production of *Rex Allen Days*, writer, and head of the *All Star Western Round-Up* tour.

Julie Ann Ream, curator of the Western Legends museum exhibit
- photo provided by Julie Ann Ream

Roy and musicians, with Cactus Mack at the piano,
In the 1939 film, The Saga of Death Valley

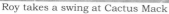
CACTUS MACK

Roy takes a swing at Cactus Mack   Cactus Mack with Tom Mix's horse, Tony Jr.

- the Rex Allen photo and all photos on this page
provided by Julie Ann Ream from her private collection

- the Dale and Buttermilk photo provided by the Rogers Family

to – Roy

I've been crazy about you all my life. Everyone kids me about it. My grown children have always made sure I saw you when you were on TV. Over the years people have ask me what my only wish would be. I always tell them to meet Roy Rogers. That's it.

Becky Strope, Bradyville, TN - 11/16/90

to – Dale

I was born in 1950 and my parents divorced when I was six years old. I lived with my mother and older sister but it didn't seem I could relate to them. My dad looked a lot like Roy and was also the quiet type, and I felt like his favorite. I would always be glued to your shows. I couldn't have gotten through those rough times without your shows. I would fantasize that my dad was Roy and you were my mother. I'm sure that many kids did the same.

Janice Pearson Arenz, St. Paul, MN - 10/11/98

to – Dale

Roy was truly a great cowboy and a wonderful man and you are an elegant lady in every sense of the word. Words cannot express our thanks for what you have done for people everywhere.

Eva Ulmer, Temple City, CA - 10/5/98

to – Roy

This is the first time I have ever tried to write you even though I have loved you since I was a little kid. I grew up watching your movies and TV shows. You were my hero and I tried to be just like you. When my mother gave me my first dog I named him after your "Bullet". But he was Bulldog, not a German shepherd. He lived 14 ½ years, and it broke my heart when he died. I know how you felt when you lost your Bullet. I also wanted a horse like Trigger, but I never lived where I could keep a horse. However, I had a rocking horse and I would rock on him with my white cowboy hat and toy guns and spend hours pretending I was you. When I was not doing that, I was reenacting one of your movies with my toy cowboys, one of which looked like you. I still have some of them. When I grew up, I put away my playthings, but I never forgot the Christian principles you and Dale Evans taught me. Give Dale my love.
David Berryman, Muscle Shoals, AL - 9/30/96

to – Roy

THEN (11/14/90): As a little girl I had a Roy Rogers bedspread, curtains and rug, a complete cowboy outfit, and a stick horse called Trigger. At supper I ate from an old pie tin like the cowboys in your movie did—hash and beans being the best. If I wouldn't eat, my grandma would tell me that Roy Rogers liked it. That did the trick! You were my hero then and you still are after all these years.

NOW (6/21/11): When Roy died a part of me died with him.
Barbara Mayer, Saginaw, MI

to – Roy and Dale

Songs for my heroes…one for Roy, one for Dale…

"Roy, You're Still a Hero to Me"   &

Roy, you're still a hero to me
Dale, you're still my favorite country
queen
Songs of the Sons of the Pioneers
Is still sweet music to my ears
And, Roy, you're still a hero to me

Worked all week long a-draggin' a sack
In the cotton patch with an achin' back
And those worn-out gloves sure made
my fingers sore
Saturday evening came around,
we'd all dress up and go to town
Got a dollar apiece and a ticket to the
picture show

Roy, you're still a hero to me
Dale, you're still my favorite country
queen
Gabby Hayes, Bullet and Pat
The good guys always wore white hats
And, Roy, you're still a hero to me

Well it don't seem that long ago
Eatin' buttered popcorn at the show
Shootin' spitballs and teasin' all the
girls
But you can bet we settled down when
they turned the show lights down
We'd set back and wait for happy trails

Roy, you're still a hero to me
Dale, you're still my favorite country
queen
Super highways are a-getting' bigger
But you know, I sure miss Trigger
Yes, Roy, you're still a hero to me

"Uvalde Honey"   by Harley Davis

She's my Uvalde Honey
She makes my cloudy days seem sunny
And Bill Gates money could never take
me away
And make me stray from my Uvalde
Honey

The purple sage is in the bloom
The fragrance fills the air
The wajia and cat claw
Bee's buzzing everywhere
They're gathering the nectar
So the Queen Bee might get chummy
But nothing in this whole wide world
Is as sweet as my Uvalde Honey

She's my Uvalde Honey
She makes my cloudy days seem sunny
And Bill Gates money could never take
me away
And make me stray from my Uvalde
Honey

Ole Cactus Jack, Roy Rogers, Dolf
Brisco
And lots of other men
Have found the place that the honey
flows
And paradise begins

But if you like wild city girls
You might think I'm kinda funny
'Cause she's angel shy, but she's still
my sweet Uvalde Honey

Harley Davis, Camp Wood, TX

---

to – Roy

You meant so much to me growing up. Both my parents were alcoholics, but you were my mainstay. I never smoked, or drank, thanks to you!

G.S. – no address – 12/12/90

---

to – Dale

You are in my thoughts daily. At nine years old I used to go to the movies on Saturday afternoon after I had cleaned my bedroom. I wore my cowgirl outfit, skirt, blouse, vest, boots and hat. At the theater before they would let me be seated they had me check in my guns (play guns of course.) I wish you and Roy could have been the First Lady and President of the United States.

Jeri Randrup, Soquel, CA - 2/7/99

to – Roy

You have been a part of my life since the first day I saw you on the silver screen in the early 1940s. I believe I have seen all your movies, either in the theater or on television. My favorite leading lady was Dale Evans, and as the years have shown, she became your favorite leading lady, too. I was born in 1934, and the females in my family loved going to the movies. When I was big enough to sit still, my mother started taking me to the old Nile Theater in Bethlehem, PA, where I was born. In the early and mid 40s I lived in Bound Brook, NJ where my family home was built by my grandfather in 1892. Every Saturday there meant a matinee with Roy and Dale. When I became an adult, I wrote to "Roy and Dale" and sent photos of my family, but my photos were returned to me with a note that said they worried that I might be sorry later on that I had parted with my precious pictures. My very best wishes and a huge thank you for all you and Dale have meant in my life. All my wishes are sent with the greatest respect and love.

Joan Blyth, Princeton, NJ - 9/27/96

> **to – Roy**
>
> You have been an excellent example of a citizen, Christian, husband and family man. I still cherish an autographed picture of you and Trigger that I've had since I was seven years old. I don't think I could live without it.
>
> *Yvonne Alber, Hato Rey, Puerto Rico* - 11/13/90

to – Roy

I'm among the luckiest of your fans because I had the chance to meet you at the Valley Ho Hotel in Scottsdale, Arizona where I worked at the desk when you were there promoting your restaurants. You were so gracious despite the fact that you were on crutches due to a tendon problem suffered at the bowling alley. (1968 maybe?) I have your picture and one of you with my father, Joe Dambrova, who worked as assistant manager at the hotel. I'm enclosing a newspaper clipping from our local paper. I thought you'd like it. Our paper isn't that big and no "local" news merits this much space! See? You're a VIP *EVERYWHERE*! And you're a VIP in the truest sense of the word!

Betsy Edwards, Victoria, TX - 10/25/90

Roy Rogers with Joe Dambrova at the Valley Ho Hotel 1960s   Roy Rogers photo autographed to Betsy (Dambrova) Edwards

- photos provided by Betsy Edwards

Essay

I love Roy Rogers and Dale Evans! I was born in 1944, and my first memories include cowgirl outfits and western toys—all Roy Rogers.

My memory of childhood friends is always playing "Roy Rogers." Every Saturday was "Pack of Fun Club" at the theater, with a Roy Rogers movie on the screen. And Trigger! I think my heart still beats a little faster when I see that beautiful, smart horse.

I never outgrew these heroes because they shared their personal lives and Christian faith with us. Roy floated down the Red River through Alexandria, Louisiana in the mid-fifties and signed autographs for hundreds of children on the riverbanks. My daddy had given me Roy and Dale's book, *The Answer is God*. When I handed Roy the book to sign he told the crowd the importance of God in their lives and to go to church and Sunday school regularly. Wow!! My hero was telling me the same thing my parents were saying! From that moment on, I was on my Christian journey.

My children and grandchildren love Roy, too. Our family room is filled with old and new memorabilia. My first grandson learned the word "Trigger" before he learned the word "horse." Some of my collection is up high and can't be played with until the children are older. One day, the boys asked me, "When you die can we have your Roy Rogers toys and movies? I said, "Yes, I want you to have them." They were quiet for a minute then one asked, "Grandmama, is it going to be a long, long time?" We got a good laugh out of that!

I have tried to pass down what Roy and Dale meant to me in my life, and especially why they are my heroes. In my heart I am forever ten years old when I hear their names. They never disappointed me, and I can always be very proud to say, "I am the greatest Roy Roger and Dale Evans fan ever.

Betty Spinks Bales, Monroe, LA - 9/9/03

Roy Rogers and Dale Evans décor in the home of Betty Spinks Bales
- photos provided by Betty Spinks Bales

---

to – Roy

I've been a fan of yours since I could turn on a television. At 25 years
old, I'm still a fan, and my nieces and nephews (and someday my own kids) will
be, too! Take care of you!

Mark St. Amand, McCordsville, IN - 11/6/90

---

to – Roy

Back in 1951, at the age of 10, I considered myself your most adored fan. In my mind, you were the epitome of life. My entire world revolved around Roy Rogers. During the week I'd wear uniforms to school, but on weekends, (the only time I felt completely dressed,) one would find me wearing my RR gun and holster set, and I would never be without my cowboy hat. The large woods behind our home was, of course, the grazing area for my horse Rusty (a two-wheel bicycle.) I envied my two brothers and all the boys in the neighborhood for their gender. Why did I have to be a girl? Your representation of the "good guys" swayed me to try to be good as well. Your love for "Gabby" Hayes inspired me to respect my elders. I remember going to the corner candy store to purchase bubble gum. Inside the little Roy Rogers gum wrappers would be lists of do's and don'ts for successful living. I would try to live according to your advice. You were a great influence on many young people, not the least of whom was me. Those were, indeed, the good old days. As the years pass, so, too, do your childhood fancies. I must admit, however, that not too long ago, while on a trip to California, I found myself outside Grauman's Chinese Theater, standing above your handprint and Trigger's hoof print, imprinted back in 1949. As I stood there, clutching the hand of my six-year-old daughter, Bonnie, all those childhood memories raced through my mind, and I couldn't help but think, 'oh what a shame Bonnie didn't grow up during my generation.' As Mr. Hope would say, thanks for the memories. With tomboy affection...

Jean (Selby) Leonard, Baltimore, MD - 11/14/90

to – Dale

I wrote the song, "The King of the Cowboys is Gone" after Roy passed away. I've been performing it ever since, and there's been a great response from my audiences. Losing Roy is hard, but he lives on in the hearts of so many.

"The King of the Cowboys is Gone" by Ted Newman

The king of the cowboys is gone
But we'll always remember his song
When we hear happy trails, we'll think of ole Roy
Remember the man called the king of the cowboys

He'd ride 'cross that silver screen
He was tough, he was honest, but he never was mean
He knew how to treat folks, he knew right from wrong
Now the King of the Cowboys is gone

On Saturdays we would all go
Down to the movies to the matinee show
We'd cheer for the man who rode Trigger, of course,
'Cause he was our hero on that big golden horse

We'd rush home to act out the show
With our Roy Rogers cap guns away we would go
On old broomstick horses with hearts that were straw
Now the King of the Cowboys is gone

Now Dale has to say adios
To the cowboy that she loved the most
They showed us the west and they gave us their best
With never a brag or a boast

"You've Made Me a Better Man" CD with song,
"The King of the Cowboys is Gone"

Ted Newman

The memories will always live on
And the things that they did and the words of their song
One day they will ride once again side-by-side
Now the King of the Cowboys is gone

The king of the cowboys is gone
But we'll always remember his song
When we hear happy trails, we'll think of ole Roy
Remember the man called the king of the cowboys

He'd ride 'cross that silver screen
He was tough, he was honest, but he never was mean
He knew how to treat folks, he knew right from wrong
Now the King of the Cowboys is gone
Yeah, the King of the Cowboys is gone

Ted Newman, Gilbert, AZ - 3/18/99

Dear Ted Newman,

Thank you for your great song! "The King of the Cowboys is Gone" – It is just beautiful and I plan to play it on my "A Date With Dale" show on T.B.N. on a Father's Day program. God bless you, Ted, in all that really counts.

Sincerely, Dale Evans Rogers

1999 Dale Evans letter to Ted Newman
- CD cover and letter from Dale provided by Ted Newman

to – Roy

I am 45 years old now but I remember when I would get up in the mornings to go to school. Roy Rogers and Gene Autry Theater would come on at 7:00 am every morning. On the mornings that Roy Rogers would be on, my mother had no problem getting me up. I wanted to be ready for school by 6:55 am so that I could watch my favorite show. The school bus picked me up at 8:05 am. Oh how I hated the mornings the bus came early. My favorite part was when you and Dale rode off into the sunset. You and Dale made me a better person. Roy Rogers will always be one of the all time greats in my eyes.

Emily Allen, LaGrange, GA - 11/7/90

to – Roy

I have never written to a famous person before but when I was a kid during World War II, going to the local theatre on Saturday afternoon to see one of your movies was just about the best part of the whole week. Me and the other kids got to see two shoot-em-up westerns, a cartoon, a short subject, world news and coming attractions and our mothers got an entire afternoon of peace and quiet, all for the price of one dime. Had to be one of the bargains of the century! A long time ago when General Douglas MacArthur addressed the Congress, he told them that old soldiers never die. They just fade away. Well, western heroes are sort of like that except for one thing, they never die AND they never fade away because they live in the hearts of their fans forever.

Ronn Faught, Glendora, CA - 11/8/90

to – Roy

Everyone has their heroes, and you and Dale have always been mine. My fondest wish is to be able to meet you two. Cowboy fans everywhere need you. We all love you. My biggest mistake of my life was not going to Apple Valley when I lived in California before moving to Montana in 1970. After that I never had the chance. Any old Roy Rogers film brings back so many childhood memories—memories never to be lost. God bless Roy and Dale.

Sandy Rose, Hamilton, MT - 11/15/90

to – Roy

THEN (10/4/96): Your fans need someone like you to look up to. I wish you had your very own TV network. I still got my Roy Rogers western tie with your picture on it with Trigger and Dale Evans, and I got your western book, King of the Cowboys" by Whitman. It's copyright 1956. I will always treasure my Roy Rogers tie and my Roy Rogers book, along with my Roy Rogers sheriff's badge, guns and other special memories.

NOW (6/14/11): I met Roy and Dale at the Shriner's Hospital. They were with Gene Autry. All of them were down to earth people who were always nice to everyone no matter who you were. I was a very lucky kid to meet them, and it was my greatest thrill. I thank the good Lord for giving us Roy and Dale, and Gene Autry, too.

Ronald Palago, Pocatello, ID

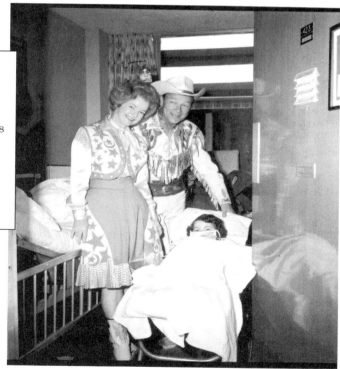

Roy Rogers and Dale Evans at Texas Children's Hospital in 1968 - photo by James de Leon, Texas Children's Hospital provided with permission

to – Dale

We had scheduled a vacation to Phoenix and California many weeks prior to Roy's death but then I arranged our driving trip to coincide with his funeral. Our boys, ages 15 and 13, know who Roy and Dale are by name, but nothing of your history, so I wanted to change that. Unfortunately, we arrived into Victorville on that Sunday evening, a day late. We made it to the museum around 4:25 pm and a nice lady at the desk noted that the museum was closed, but she let us make a quick run inside just to let us take a photo of our two boys in front of Trigger. Dusty heard of our story and offered to give us directions to the gravesite. Out in the parking lot we started talking to a gentleman dressed in a western outfit. He told us he was from San Diego and felt moved to make the trip to the funeral, telling us that he entertained the many who waited in line to get into the museum with his rope tricks. I forgot his name, but he really made us feel so welcome, like we were part of the family. He was also heading in our same direction. As we arrived closer to the cemetery, we were so impressed by the beauty of that area. You really picked a spot as close to what Heaven must look like! At the grave site, we talked to another dozen or more of your and Roy's fans. Patty purchased a book of beautiful poems and we just had a wonderful time meeting so many special people at a most reverent place. I guess I wanted to let you know how much you and Roy meant to my wife and I growing up in the 50s, and now our boys know the importance of Roy Rogers and Dale Evans. You both are the very essence of the moral makeup of our society. You will leave this earth knowing that when you meet God, you will be smiling with a confidence that you both truly inspired and moved the American people (and millions of people from other countries, too) to do our very best to raise our families in the most wholesome manner. Thank you for your time and courtesy. My regrets in life are few – getting my family closer to Victorville was worth every minute we spent. May God bless you with many more years here on earth to spread His message. I finish this letter hoping you know that we got *YOUR* message.
Steve, Patty, Kyle and Erik Durant, Midlothian, VA - 11/9/98

to – Dale

I've wanted to write to you since I heard of the passing of Mr. Rogers. My only regret is that I didn't write the letter while he was still alive so that he could know my feelings also. I grew up on your movies and TV shows as so many did, but I need you to know that it had far more of an impact than just entertainment. I'd play with my friends, and I always wanted to be Roy. Being young without true gender concept, I just knew I wanted to be the one who stood for the right thing and stopped the bad guy. Well, that's just what I made the decision to do with my life. I am an R.N. and have been working in the medical field for over 30 years. Currently I am the Night Hospital Supervisor at Sharp Hospital Murietta, right across the street from the proposed "Rogersdale". So, much like a vigilant sheriff, I patrol my town at night to keep her, and all in her, safe. With God's help and guidance I do my best. I don't believe I would ever have had that spiritual or moral conviction without the example you gave that I grew up with. I thank you from the bottom of my heart.

Lucy Doty, Lake Elsinore, CA - 11/12/98

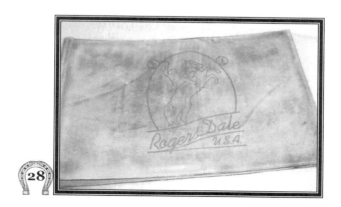

to – Roy

"Lord, but you had a lot of action in those films of yours. You really upset a lot of "Bad Apples" in those days. As my hero, you were "A-1

Gary of NH - 11/10/90

to – Roy

THEN (11/7/90): I have been a fan of yours for 45 years. You, more than any other man, molded my values as a child and as an adult. I sense that some of my most difficult lessons are still to be learned, and I still need you as a model to show me the way. I wish there was something I could do for you to repay you for all you have done for me. I will, of course, pray for you always."

NOW (8/14/11): I am now seventy years old and have been a fan of Roy Rogers for as long as I can remember. He taught me some of my basic, lifelong-held beliefs, like 'it's more fun to be good' and 'if you choose to do something, do it to the best of your abilities.' I read every one of his books and remember how he liked using disguises. He once pretended to be an old-time mountain man, but he knew that to pull it off he had to fake eating with his fingers and a knife. But he doubted his ability to fake such idiosyncrasies so he decided to use a spoon for everything. His lesson to me in that book was 'there is always a way, we just have to think and use our brains and not just a six-gun.' That was one lesson that saved me many times in my life. Another lesson that has worked for me was 'everyone should have his own curse phrase.' I even remember the one he used, and he said we could use it, too, if we wanted—namely: "You slimy little cheap john, tin horn, buster faced, little plaster." Or: "You weasel jawed, fish eyed little runt." It wasn't until years later that I studied about the value of catharsis, as in "Deal with it then let it go, and move on." Without Roy's wisdom, I would have clogged up years ago. I wept when he died."
Blaine Bethune, Regina, Saskatchewan, Canada

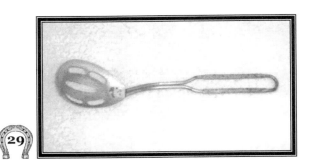

29

Roy Rogers was my childhood hero. I wrote him fan letters every week when I was young. Nothing thrilled me more than hearing back from him, which I did several times. I still have a beloved 8x10 picture of Roy and Trigger, that Roy inscribed to me when I was a little girl, hanging in my office.

When I was young I dreamed of being a cowboy, just like Roy. When I was older and learned more about Roy, Dale, their children, and all the good work they did, they became even bigger heroes to me. I have always been inspired by their integrity, their generosity, their faith, their humility, and their commitment to doing right.

Several years ago, when I had a licensing company to handle "Cathy" merchandise, I had the chance to represent Roy Rogers merchandising for a period of time. There was interest in developing a new TV series or movie to introduce Roy to the next generation, as well as a movement to revive some of the classic images on products for those of us who grew up with Roy. It was the thrill of my life to get to meet Roy and Dale at their museum one day, and to get to feel that my company might be able to help bring some new attention to them.

Ultimately, the people trying to develop the TV and movie projects failed to get very far, and the association came to a close, but I left the experience feeling amazingly blessed that I'd gotten to be a tiny bit close to someone who had always been, and will always be, a shining role model for me.

Roy and Dale had (and still have) a huge impact on my life.

Cathy Guisewite, Cartoonist and Creator of the "Cathy" Cartoon Strip

The hand-drawn "Cathy" card created especially for Dale Evans
and Cartoonist Cathy Guisewite with Roy Rogers
- photo and card art provided with permission by Cathy Guisewite

to – Roy

THEN (10/7/96): I've wanted to write to you for over 40 years. I want you to know just what you have meant to me. In 1948 I was 10 years old, and you were my hero. I lived near Coloma, California. I learned that you were to be grand marshal at the California Gold Centennial, and I was determined to finally meet the man and his horse that meant so much to me. The magic moment came, but the cars were lined up for miles, and it was impossible to drive there. My father wouldn't wait in the line, but he did give my brother and I permission to walk there if we wanted to. It was more than five miles of walking (what a wonderful time that was, when children could go someplace alone without fear.) There I was in the front row in front of your trailer, and at last you appeared. But I got tongue-tied. I never got to talk to you or get your autograph. It was probably the only time in my life I was at a loss for words, and in my whole life I never wanted anyone else's autograph. By that time you had already been my hero for a long time, for as long as I could remember, really. Your "Code of the West" became my code. I ate, slept, walked and talked Roy and Trigger. I was a little jealous of Dale, as she ruined my plans to grow up and marry you, but later I couldn't imagine you without her. The life lessons I absorbed from my fascination and love for you and Dale and Trigger have stayed with me all my life. They helped shape my character and sense of honor and faithful steadfastness, and even today, if given the choice of meeting any famous person, I would choose you. I've never forgotten you, and even as you and Dale reach the sunset of your lives, you are like flesh and blood parents and grandparents to so many of us. I may never get your autograph or get to meet you in person, but I'll see you in Heaven, and I'll hear God say, "Well done, thou good and faithful servant." I am a fan for life. You have my love and my prayers.

NOW (8/3/11): "Roy's "Code of the West" is timeless—*You don't start a fight, but you don't walk away from one. You always defend the underdog, stand up for what's right, don't lie, always keep your word, and you don't ever give up.* I've lived those life lessons, and I never quit loving Roy and Dale. As a grown up there was only "one person" I would have gone out of my way to meet among all the Hollywood stars and that was Roy and Dale, who I came to think of as one. My whole philosophy of life was based on the code I learned from Roy, and I've never regretted a minute of being that kind of person. I'm 73 years old today and still riding the range on a cattle ranch in North Dakota, 50 miles from town, and still loving my dream come true."

Karen Meyer, Solen, ND

Roy Rogers and Dale Evans
- photo provided by the Rogers Family

to – Roy

It is truly an honor to be able to write to you and tell you how much I enjoyed your movies and TV shows back in the 1950s and 1960s. I have been a fan of yours for virtually my entire 42 years. When I was in grade school I used to hurry home after basketball practice to see "Circle-2 Theatre"—one Roy Rogers movie and one Gene Autry movie back to back. Then, of course, Saturdays soon featured the Roy Roger's Show and "Happy Trails to You!" In all my life I can honestly say I've only had 3 heroes—St Francis of Assisi, Roy Rogers and Rocky Marciano. I always felt St. Francis was a special person because he was kind to, and cared about, animals. Rocky was a tough, rugged guy in the boxing ring, but gentle and decent to the public. And of course, to me, Roy Rogers was a combination of these qualities—gentle to animals (Trigger, Buttermilk, Bullet, etc.,) and righteous in the just and noble sense, but with a good left uppercut & right-hand sock for the bad guys—if and when it was *really* deserved. I always admired that blend of decency and toughness, and I attribute, in large part, my activism in the animal-help and environmental movements to the seeds of justice planted in my mind while watching Roy, Trigger, and the gang. In your movies your most common sidekick was Gabby Hayes: "By-Willikers!" "Dagnabbit!" "Jumpin' Gee-Hossifat!" He was a character the world has never seen the likes of since! And I came to love the beautiful and always-concerned Dale, Pat Garret and Nellybelle, the always-sleek Bullet, the dependable Buttermilk, and the equine "Clark Gable"—Trigger! Those were some of the nicest times of my life, and I want to thank you and Dale for making it a wonderful time to grow up. So much of the attitudes and feelings in my life are a direct result of my youthful admiration for Roy Rogers and Dale Evans and the way you treated people, animals and each other. I would also like to share a poem I wrote on my 17th birthday, a day that I will never forget.

"The Day That Trigger Died" by Stephen F. McCormick

Sometimes fate is oh so sad
I remember when I cried,
July the 3rd of '65
The day that Trigger died

I loved that Palomino
That big, strong, handsome steed,
Roy Rogers' friend, so loyal and smart
So noble, with such speed

His sculpted body dipped in gold
White flowing mane and tail,
Part of a team who fought for good
He sped down many trails

Animals, they are my friends
Cats, dogs, etcetera
But Trigger was a "special friend"
For many kids, I'll bet ya!

A true friend's there through thick and thin,
That's the truest test
'Ole Trigger never let Roy down,
He was the best friend in the West

"Silver," "Topper," and "Champion"
These were great mounts, too,
And helped the Lone Ranger, Hoppy and Gene
Give the bad guys their due

But ears and mane above these greats
Trigger pranced and reared,
And when he chased the outlaws down,
We little wranglers cheered!

This equine hero was our friend
There throughout the years,
His passing was a chapter closed,
We said "Goodbye" with tears

July the 3rd of '65
The day that Trigger died,
It was my birthday - 17
But I just sat and cried.

I may not have loved Trigger as dearly as you, Roy, but I'm guessing it was pretty close. I loved and admired him, and I love and admire you. I wish you health and happiness—the kind of happiness you so freely and generously inspired in others throughout the world. You deserve to be remembered, and it will always be so. Happy Trails to you and yours, Roy...forever and a day!
Stephen F. McCormick, Antigo, WI - 11/9/90

Roy Rogers and Trigger
- photo provided by the Rogers Family

to – Dale

I remember seeing you and Roy and your kids in Des Moines, Iowa, probably in 1960 or 1961, at the Iowa State Fair. I was about 5 years old. Some people who went to see your show were told they could meet you in person after the show, but evidently *you* hadn't been told that! So as you were driving away, a father from another family waved Roy down, and we all just had a chance to say hello to you before you drove away. I still remember that—Roy in his cowboy hat and you in a white stole. Then several years ago I read your book, *Angel Unaware*, and have recently looked and looked for my copy. An 85-year-old man drops by for a visit at the office of my Christian newspaper, *The City Gate*, quite frequently. He has a great-granddaughter who was born with problems but who is a complete joy to their whole family. This gentleman also read your book but cannot find his copy either, and he would like for his grandson and his wife to read it. We are both hoping the book is still available, and I thank you in advance for letting me know if it is. I have wondered how to get in contact with you, and then today saw you on TBN. God works in mysterious ways – His wonders to perform. Thank you so much!

Michelle Fetters Steen, Indianola, IA - 9/19/98

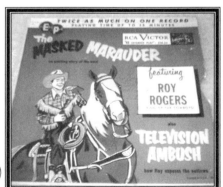

to – Dale

After several months and much frustration on trying to win bids on eBay® for an autographed picture of my favorite stars, I have thrown in the towel. I figured what the heck. Why not just write and ask for one. The worst that could happen is that you throw my letter in the trash, right? So here I am, SASE enclosed. I do so hope to see that brown envelope show up in my mailbox with that much-hoped-for photo inside. And I thank you so much. I also want to express my deepest sympathy on the loss of your husband. You and he were, and are, loved by so many dedicated fans. You will both be in our hearts always. We love you!

Debbie Cheseldine, Mt. Airy, MD - 2/3/99

to – Roy

You are like an old friend of the family to me. I love you for what you represent—a down-to-earth, good person, a good actor, and a good, moral family man. I remember going to the Strand Theater in Waynesboro, Pennsylvania on Friday and Saturday nights in the late 1940s. And more than 40 years later, in 1985, it was a thrill to shake your hand at the opening of your new Roy Rogers restaurant in Ellicott City. Even today I look forward to watching and listening to the videos and CDs I have of you and Dale. With much love and admiration, I wish you all things wonderful.

Ann Stoops, Gaithersburg, MD - 11/8/90

Essay

Nudie the Rodeo Tailor and Roy Rogers
- photo provided by Jamie Nudie

My story...

I can think of many ways to express my feelings toward Roy and Dale, but a few thoughts stand out on their own. Nudie and Bobbie, my grandparents, were not merely the designers of Roy and Dale's clothing. They were family friends.

I can remember all the times when The Rogers' came into Nudie's Rodeo Tailor's and just sat around talking about all the good times they shared. In fact my most heartfelt story is when Nudie passed in 1984 and Dale spoke for his eulogy. I had written an open letter to my grandfather and when Dale read it, she read it with such expression that even I was in tears. She also sang at his graveside.

My mother, Barbara, the only daughter to the Nudie family, passed away in 1990 at the young age of 52. Dale was off doing a ministry, but Roy, knowing we had no men in the family, stood by my grandmother and I during such a difficult time.

Roy stood in my living room holding a plate of food amongst all the friends who had attended the service, and I will never forget seeing that sparkle in his eyes, as he was not just Roy Rogers, the King of the Cowboys. He was family.

I can always remember hearing the stories my grandparents would share with me on how Roy and Dale were not just clients, but how they became and stayed family friends. In fact, Nudie and Roy were so close that Nudie gave Roy one if his Nudie mobiles and trailer as a gift.

Much later, I had the honor of buying back that trailer to keep that friendship alive in all their memories. I know that Nudie and Bobbie, Roy and Dale are now sitting around reminiscing on all the great times they shared together while on earth. I am so happy to have been part of the history of Roy and Dale!

Jamie Nudie, Nudie's Rodeo Tailors – co-author of *Nudie the Rodeo Tailor: The Life and Times of the Original Rhinestone Cowboy*

Roy Rogers and Nudie check out new boots

Roy Rogers and Nudie the Rodeo Tailor
in a sea of clothes made for Roy by Nudie

Jamie Nudie with an original Nudie
Mobile and the Trailer given to
Roy Rogers and Dale Evans
by Nudie the Rodeo Tailor

– all photos provided by Jamie Nudie

to – Dale

My name is Margaret Usher, and I live in Belize City, Belize, in Central America. I have watched TBN for some time now, and was amazed to see you on it. Here I am, always loving you and Roy as my heroes, and now, to learn that you are both Christians, it's just so wonderful. Oh how I love that. I may not get to meet you, but we'll meet in Heaven some day. I love writing to you. You are always so nice and cheerful and happy, and sometimes I feel down and depressed, and you just seem so "motherly." I guess sometimes I just need a little word of wisdom and encouragement and to be set on the right track. I've always wanted to write but was a little scared. Anyway, I've always loved both you and Roy, and I thank God for you.

Margaret Usher, Belize City, Belize, Central America - 9/20/98

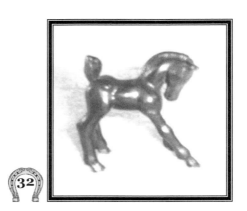

to – Roy

Oh how I enjoyed your shows growing up, and I still have my Roy Rogers and Dale Evans lunch box! I am 41 years old and cherish growing up with you. Please take care of yourself, and give my best to Dale. God bless.

Kathleen Wagner, Tunkhannock, PA - 11/19/90

to – Roy

We all love you and need more people like you and Dale in this world. You both have given us so much happiness. I am 81 years old, and I've seen all your movies. I've lived in Cincinnati since I was born and tell people from out of town that you are from Cincinnati, too. We are all so proud of you. My husband and I were married 54 years when he passed away 7 years ago, and I still miss him so much. Roy, you are so lucky to have such a wonderful wife as Dale. She really is a beautiful woman. A few years ago my family and I got a chance to visit your museum. We really enjoyed it. I only wish I had bought something from there. People are so thrilled to meet you at the museum. The children today miss so much not being able to watch you and Dale and Gene Autry. Those were pictures you could enjoy with your kids. I say a prayer every morning and night for you and Dale. I wish we could have met you two when we were there. That really would have made our day. I sure hope my grandchildren and great-grandchildren get to come out to your museum. Just remember, Roy, if there were more people like you to for the young people, they might be different. My granddaughter said to tell you how you saved her son's life. When he was 3 ½ months old he died in her arms 3 times, and once more at the hospital. He had a very serious heart operation that the doctors said they only do once or twice a year. She was told he would need a heart transplant also. He got so much better after taking a lot of medicine. He is now 3 ½ years old, off of all medicine, and is doing fine. When Pam brought him home he couldn't sleep. He would cry all the time until she played your music and Garth Brook's music. He would then drift off to sleep. She played your music until it burnt up, and she had to get another one. He loved "Happy Trails." You and Dale really helped him. Pam named him Garth. Garth still listens to your music and sings along with you. He knows every word. We told him how you saved his life and that I was sending you a letter, and he said, "Tell Roy Rogers and Dale Evans I love them for saving my life." Pam also sends her thanks and hopes she can get out there with Garth to meet you. Roy, God loves you, and so do I.

Ruth Wendt, Williamsburg, OH - 10/7/96

to – Roy

In April, 1989, my children and I met you at your museum. That was one happy day, even though I was crying (tears of happiness!) That day my prayers had been answered. I so treasure that memory and the pictures we had taken with you. I have thought about you so many times throughout my life. I try to imagine what your life must be like and what you might be doing at some particular moment in time. How I would love to see you again and talk with you. When I happen to see you on TV I really do go bonkers, and my kids say, "Are you going to cry?" And I usually do. The actor, Wilford Brimley, lives in our town, only about a mile from us. I sure wish you lived here, too. It would be so great seeing you out and about, at church or in town. But wherever you live and whatever you do, Happy Trails to you!

Myrna Daly, Lehi, UT - 11/2/90

to – Dale

To say that Roy Rogers was loved by generations of kids is putting it mildly. He was a guidepost for those of us who chose to live good, decent lives. His handsome good looks, his sense of morality and fair play, touched me in a way that remained with me all of my life. And I love the song Dusty wrote for Roy. The words are a wonderful tribute to his dad. Thank you and God bless you.

Cookie Curci, San Jose, CA - 9/8/98

King of the Cowboys – Roy "Dusty" Rogers, Jr.

He's rode across your silver screen
For over 60 years
He's brought bad men to justice
He's seen laughter and he's seen tears

And I know forever
In many a heart he will reign
As the King of the Cowboys
There is honor to his name

He's a kind and gentle legend
A hero is his fame
Showing young folks to see the right from wrong
And he's taught me the very same

And I know forever
In many hearts he'll reign
As the King of the Cowboys
There is magic to his name

He's the King of the Cowboys
A legend in his time
A man who loved this country
Where he will always ride

Saddled up on his golden Palomino
With a six gun by each side
In his boots and spurs and his white hat
Rides a man with a lot of pride

And I know forever
That in many hearts he'll reign
As the King of the Cowboys
There is honor to his name

He's the King of the Cowboys
A legend in his time
A man who loved this country
Where he will always ride

Riding off into the sunset
In a western sky of blue
He has given us precious memories
And "Happy Trails" for me and you

Roy Rogers, Dale Evans, Roy "Dusty" Rogers, Jr.
- photo provided by the Rogers Family

Roy Rogers and Dusty Rogers
learning the ropes

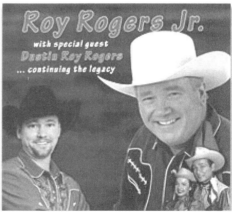

Roy "Dusty" Rogers, Jr. CD with song
"King of the Cowboys" and special guest artist
Dusty's son, Dustin Roy Rogers

- photos provided by the Rogers Family

to – Roy

I am severely handicapped, unable to walk since birth, with cerebral palsy. But from the time I was quite young, you and Dale have given me many hours of enjoyment over the years. Just check out that Roy and Trigger on my TV! I am 44 years old now. God bless you, Roy.

Wayne Ingalls, Machias, ME - 11/7/90

1955 -Wayne Ingalls
with Roy Rogers and Trigger on TV
       1989 – Wayne Ingalls

- photos provided by Wayne Ingalls

to – Dale

Even though you might never meet me, I feel I know you as well as my own mother. All my love to you and your family.

Deborah L. Guynn, Bowie, MD - 12/17/98

to – Dale

We are planning a vacation weekend in the area and will be at the museum on March 29. I have a very old advertisement, from the 60s I believe. It describes the Roy Rogers Apple Valley Inn with rates of $50 per person for a whole week! I wondered if you would like to add it to other advertisements in the museum. It would be our pleasure to give it to you when we come. We recently enjoyed the Sons of the Pioneers at the Tucson Triple "C" Chuck Wagon. It was just wonderful! We're sorry to have missed Dusty though. Our love goes out to you and all the family. We are devoted fans and are so looking forward to our vacation to the museum.

Ethelene and Bob Henze, Tucson, AZ – 3/3/99

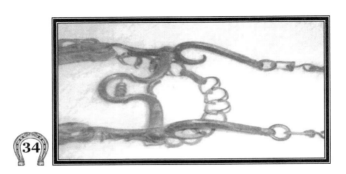

to – Roy and Dale

We're just two of your many fans who wish the best for you. We have seen and visited with you several times in Victorville, and each time we enjoy it more. The last time we were early, and Roy, you and Dusty were busy changing one of the booths. We so appreciated you both taking the time to talk with us even though you were busy. It meant a lot to us. And when you asked if we would like pictures taken with you, it really made our day. Your museum is great. So much love surrounds everyone there. The things you have are precious memories for you, but for all who visit there, too. Take care always.

Lester and Louise Potts, Washington, KS - 10/9/96

Essay

To this day we receive letters from Gene Autry fans, who, growing up in the 1940s and 1950s, would take the role of their favorite western character, Gene or Roy. It was a friendly rivalry fueled in part by the press. However, the truth was, Gene and Roy enjoyed a friendship that lasted until both passed away in 1998.

Throughout the years their paths would cross at various events. Roy, Dale and family members watched the Angels play baseball from Gene's suite at Anaheim Stadium. In 1992 they were honored at the Autry Museum of Western Heritage. Gene appeared on Happy Trails Theater in the 1980s. Roy and Dale joined Gene for Melody Ranch Theater.

In 1997 Gene Autry Entertainment hosted a Gene Autry Fan Club Convention, with fans coming from as far away as New Zealand. It was a weeklong celebration of Gene Autry where fans had a chance to visit places associated with him. Among the places we visited was the Roy Rogers-Dale Evans Museum in Apple Valley. Roy was so gracious as over a hundred fans descended on the museum at once. He enjoyed visiting with the fans—so very much like Gene did. I think perhaps I was the most excited, for I had grown up with Roy and Dale and their television show. Roy very kindly spent time with me, too, and asked about Gene.

Watching Gene, Roy and Dale on the screen, you are a part of the adventure, racing with the wind and winning the day, seeing the qualities that are the best in all of us—loyalty, courage, friendship and love among them. It makes you feel that anything is possible. What a great gift to give to people.

Maxine Hansen, Executive Assistant to Mrs. Gene Autry, Gene Autry Entertainment

Roy Rogers and Gene Autry trading cowboy boots for golf shoes

Gene Autry and Roy Rogers get a kick out of the "funnies"

to – Roy

I've been mentally writing you a fan letter since your appearance on Saturday morning TV. My dad would pop into the room and remark, "Y'know, he used to come into our bar." At one time Dad (Mike,) Uncle Stan (Laszlo,) and brother-in-law Charlie owned a bar with shuffleboard. Uncle Stan was a 1934-35 Golden Gloves champ. Dad was an electrician, and Charlie was the entrepreneur. Dad also told me that Dick Powell would drop off his kids, and for $3 or $4 they were fed milk and cookies for a few hours. My neighbor knows you, too. She used to play poker with you in East Hollywood. I think these events occurred over 40 years ago, before I was born. I just loved your show. Looking back, life wasn't as complicated then. The Good Guys in the white hats only wounded the Bad Guys then brought them in for a fair trial. You were such a hero to so many kids. About 8 years ago I attended a seminar at the hospital where I work. The main idea throughout the discussions was children patterning themselves after their heroes. So we all yelled out our heroes. I yelled out "Roy Rogers!" and an African-American coworker said, "He's my hero, too!" I guess that's the true sense of a hero, someone who shines for all people. After all these years, I'm still a fan. I never gave away my Roy Rogers shirt, and I still have 78s of you and Dale singing. And when I was a kid, I would tell people my name was Stephen "Roy Rogers" Nagy. So Happy Trails to you, Roy! Happy Trails to you!

Stephen Nagy, Brisbane, CA – undated

to – Roy

THEN (11/29/90): We grew up in the 50s and watched you and Dale on TV every time you made an appearance. My husband is such a devoted fan, and your song "Happy Trails" is his favorite. As a matter of fact, he has instructed me to make sure that it is played at his funeral! He has told our children the same thing. If you are ever in the Asheville area, we would love to see you. My husband's father has a restaurant that sells home cooking, and we would take you to dinner!

Karen and Fred Embler

NOW (7/31/11): I lost Freddie unexpectedly on October 2, 2001. In the very first year of our marriage (we were married 31 years,) he told me that he wanted "Happy Trails" played at his funeral. And in 2001, as his casket was rolled out at the end of the service, "his song" was played. I stood there with a tearful smile, and his sister, Dawn, told me that it made her remember him as a child in his cowboy outfit. The legacy of Roy Rogers and Dale Evans is far beyond their work in the entertainment industry. They left many "Happy Trails" behind."

Karen Embler

Resting place of devoted fan, Freddie Embler
- photo provided by Karen Embler

143

---

to – Roy

    I loved you as a child! Mom said I was constantly running around with my brother's cowboy hat and six-shooters on. I ended up marrying a rancher, and my husband and I now have a little cowgirl and little cowboy of our own. I only wish you were still on TV for them! Thanks for all the wonderful memories!

Nancy Summerer, Ewing, NE - 11/13/90

to – Roy

    It is an honor to write to you, "My Favorite Cowboy." Every Sunday I watch your movies on TV, and I am a kid again. I got my first pony when I was 10 years old, and all I wanted was to be a cowgirl! I named my pony Silver. He was a feisty little stinker. The first time I got on him he took off running, veering into an evergreen tree, where I was promptly sent to the ground! I am now 44 and have managed to keep the "kid" in me ever alive. You can be sure my granddaughter will know you as well. Elton John sings a song entitled, "Roy Rogers," which you should keep near. I'm sending you the words to the song. I'm sure I speak for many others in saying truer words were

Sandra (Tong) White Draper leading little sister, Mary, on Silver
- photo provided by Sandra Draper

never spoken. You have brought joy to millions and always will. You are a positive influence and a truly great man. Thank you from the bottom of my heart!

Sandra (Tong) White Draper, Sturgeon Bay, WI - 11/19/90

"Roy Rogers"

Lyrics by Bernie Taupin – Music by Elton John

Sometimes you dream, sometimes it seems
There's nothing there at all
You just seem older than yesterday
And you're waiting for tomorrow to call

You draw to the curtains, and one thing's for certain
You're cozy in your little room
The carpet's all paid for, God bless the TV
Let's go shoot a hole in the moon

And Roy Rogers is riding tonight
Returning to our silver screen
Comic book characters never grow old
Evergreen heroes whose stories were told
Oh the great sequin cowboy who sings of the plains
Of roundups and rustlers and home on the range
Turn on the TV, shut out the light
Roy Rogers is riding tonight

Nine o'clock mornings, five o'clock evenings
I'd liven the pace if I could
Oh I'd rather have ham in my sandwich than cheese
But complaining wouldn't do any good

Lay back in my armchair, close eyes and think clear
I can hear hoof beats ahead
Roy and Trigger have just hit the hilltop
While the wife and the kids are in bed

Oh, and Roy Rogers is riding tonight
Returning to our silver screens
Comic book characters never grow old
Evergreen heroes whose stories were told
Oh the great sequin cowboy who sings of the plains
Of roundups and rustlers and home on the range
Turn on the TV, shut out the light
Roy Rogers is riding tonight

"Roy Rogers" song lyrics printed with permission
from Elton John and Bernie Taupin

Roy Rogers
- photo provided by the Rogers Family

to – Dale

THEN (10/21/98): I'm writing to convey my best wishes on your birthday, and I've enclosed a small donation in memory of Roy. Please use it in Roy's name for a cause dear to him and to yourself. It goes a little way in saying a BIG thank you to you and Roy for the wonderful memories. I still like to find a quiet moment to play CDs of the two of you singing the great old western songs. There are so many memories to treasure. You have my warmest wishes always."

NOW (7/13/11): I was fortunate to have had several correspondences with Roy and Dale and their daughter, Cheryl, throughout the years, and it meant so much to me. When I was a lad, Roy was a great favourite of mine. That never changed. It was a wonderful time in our youthful lives, then we grew up, and the memories and thoughts would drift back to our young days, keeping us young at heart. Gene Autry was my other great favourite, and the loss of Roy, Dale and Gene seemed to somehow endanger the link to my past as well. They were such a part of me. But that's why memories are so important. These great people will live forever in the memory of those who loved them.
Keith Harvey, Weymouth, Dorset, England

1993 - "Thank You" photo from Roy Rogers and Dale Evans to Keith Harvey
- photo provided by Keith Harvey

1995 - Roy Rogers signing cast of Trigger
- photo provided by Keith Harvey

1994 - Actor Gregg Barton, Keith Harvey, Actor Walter Reed with Roy Rogers Signature
- photo provided by Keith Harvey

1999 - Letter to Keith Harvey
from Dale Evans
- letter, (one of many,)
provided by Keith Harvey

Rc. 6TH APRL 1999

Mar 30, 1999

Dear Keith,

*Thank you for the lovely Easter card.
It must be a beautiful, green Easter in
England. In 1954 I enjoyed the
country eastern fields so much, and
the warm English folks. It was a
thrill to be there for the Billy Graham
Crusade at Harringay. May God
richly bless your life with all that
really counts for His Kingdom!*

*Sincerely in Christ, Dale Evans
Rogers*

---

to – Dale

All my boys were raised on the cowboy way of Roy Rogers and Gene
Autry, just like your children were. I only wish my grandchildren and great-
grandchildren could be so fortunate.

a fan, GA

to – Roy

Because I have always been a fan of yours, I wanted to drop you a letter and tell you how much you have meant to me over the years. As a little girl (I'm now 50) growing up in Bradenton, Florida, how I looked forward to watching the Roy Rogers show each week and hearing you sing with Dale, "Happy Trails," at the end of the show. I had several of your records and would play them over and over. What a joy you brought into my childhood. As I have been writing to you I have been trying to remember the one song you sang that meant so much to me. The last two verses had such an impact on me. It went like this:

So let the sunshine in
Face it with a grin
Smilers never lose, and
Frowners never win

So let the sunshine in
Face it with a grin
Open up your heart and
Let the sunshine in

When you forget to say your prayers
The devil jumps with glee
But he feels so awful, awful
When he sees you on your knees

So when you're full of troubles
And you never seem to win
Just open up you heart
And let the sunshine in

I would sing this song over and over. Because my dad did not live with us, my sweet mom had many struggles raising three children alone, but we would all sing your song and know that God would take care of us. However, my mom and dad did get together to take my sister and I to the Tampa State Fair to see you perform. I wore my only pair of jeans and cowboy boots for the special occasion, and what a thrill it was for me. It was a day I will never forget. Thank you for helping plant the seed of God's love in my heart. Even though I have never had the opportunity of meeting you face to face, please know you will always have a place in my heart. God bless you.
Toni Winslett, Loganville, GA - 10/22/96

---

to – Roy and Dale

I wish I knew how to yodel! But, I figure when we all get to Heaven, you'll teach us. You will, won't you?
a fan, WA – 9/27/96

to – *Dale*

I am 46 years old on May 29th, but I am really around "10-to-12 young at heart," just like you and Roy Rogers. I only wish we had role models like you and Roy now. Excuse me for telling you, but Roy was my first boyfriend! I know you must hear that a lot. My husband bought me the new tape recording of Roy's favorites with new Western recording artists. I cried when I first listened to it, although I was disappointed that you were not on the recording. There is a Dale Evans song group in Texas, but it's not you! I do believe you are the best representation of the American family. I hear that Roy is giving his permission to "cartoonize" his TV series. But please suggest a VCR package of all his shows in his TV series, or at least reruns of them on cable. My children are growing up, and I am sharing Roy Rogers, Dale Evans, Trigger, Buttermilk and Bullet with them. I love you both!

Barbara Berlin, Bryn Mawr, PA - 5/15/92

to – *Roy*

Sorry it took me so long to send my well wishes and Christmas cheers. I survived a head-on collision, and I'm still trying to get the hitch out of my giddyup. But I could not miss the chance to write to you and tell you that you're Canada's favorite cowboy and mine, too! All my best wishes!"

Sue Krac, Toronto, Ontario, Canada - 12/14/90

1987 - Roy Rogers sharing a smile with Arlene Levens and her proud dad
- photo provided by Arlene Levens

to – Roy

I had the pleasure of meeting you at the museum in 1987, along with my husband, dad and stepmother. It was one of the biggest thrills of my life to actually get to meet you, and you were just as sweet and friendly as I always knew you would be. My dad started taking me to see your movies when I was 5 years old, and we have been your biggest fans ever since. I'll never forget the look on my dad's face as he shook your hand. You were making a commercial that day, and we got to see you emerge in your beautiful cowboy clothes. What a dream visit it was. We all love you so much. Thank you for the wonderful memories.

Arlene Levens, Fort Worth, TX - undated

Roy was without a doubt one of the sweetest, warmest gentlemen I have ever met, and it was amazing, being in awe of him only to find him to be just a regular guy—really nice, and so much fun! He loved playing cards and fishing. He asked me if I played Gin Rummy. I said that I'd like to learn and he taught me to play Gin Rummy, which I still play to this day.

In my wildest dreams I couldn't believe my incredible luck to play the ingénue lead in my very first movie with Roy and Dale, my screen idols. At seventeen years old I was very shy, never having been to Hollywood, much less on a movie set, and everything was so fascinating for me.

My memories of Dale are special, too. She was the cutest, spunkiest lady I had ever met. She, too, was warm and loving, and she took me under her wing, literally, taking me off the set to go shopping—with my mother's approval of course. We had a great time. Dale was so talented, and could she sing! She and Roy were just great together.

We shot the movie in October of 1947, and they were married that year on New Year's Eve.

I will never forget making my first film—playing "Rosa" in "Apache Rose"—with Roy and Dale. And I will never forget the people they were.

Donna Martell – Movie and Television Actress (Ms. Martell appears in the credits of Apache Rose as Donna DeMario)

Donna Martell

- photos provided by Donna Martell

to – Roy

I would like for you to think of all the good that you have done for others in your life. If there were more men like you for the children of today to emulate, this country would be a far better place. You, sir, were more than just an actor. You were a teacher. In all of your movies you taught us that the good guys with the white hats always win over evil. I never once went to one of your movies and heard you curse or swear. You were always courteous. You showed us young boys that you could be a real man and still be a good man. You should hold your head up high and be proud of the contributions that you've made to generations of children. You taught us to want to be one of the good guys like you. I, like millions of others, am proud of the way that you and your wife selflessly gave of yourselves. Can you imagine the joy that you will feel when Jesus calls you forward to reward you for all of the good that you have done in your lifetime? The millions of us who learned so much from you will be giving you a standing ovation with a smile on our faces and a song in our hearts. I'm a true admirer who loves you for who you are. As you always said, "Goodbye for now, and may the Good Lord take a liking to you!
Lewis Parry, Kirksville, MO - 10/11/96

to – Roy

Remember, Mr. Rogers, people come and go, but legends live forever!
Your fan, NJ

to – Roy and Dale

You two have been my heroes for over 50 years now and it's high time I let you know. When I was a little girl on my dad's farm, my older sister would say to me, "There's a Roy Rogers movie playing in town. If you ask Dad for the car, I'll take you and Larry (my neighbor and cousin) to see it." My good dad never let us down. Me missed few. I'll never forget the day my sister told me that Roy and Dale were getting married. That was too good! I thought she was just saying it to see what I would do, but it was true! It was a dream come true for two kids you loved you both. We danced and whooped and hollered. You were my heroes then, and still are to this day. I'm so happy to say that my "hero worship" for you two was well founded. There are few heroes in Hollywood. No role models. Hollywood has become a format of perversion and violence, and the people running the show take absolutely no responsibility for their young followers. God help them. I have seen some truly great artists in concert over the years, but to my great chagrin, I never got to see either of you. But glory be to God, He's fixed it so one day we can meet in Heaven, and I'm planning on spending at least 100 years in "Heaven" time just hangin' around with you and your family! Well, I've just done something I've wanted to do my whole life, and that is write to you to let you both know how very much you have touched my life, and how very much I have always loved "you'ns." God's continued blessings on both of you. Thank you both so very, *very* much. I love you to pieces! Oh, and you both have birthdays soon, so HAPPY BIRTHDAY! My birth date is 10-10-36, and talking to you in this letter is MY birthday present. YES! It's a good one! Happy Trails Roy and Dale. Happy Trails!

Ellie Fuller, Wooster, OH - 10/9/96

I saw my first Roy Rogers Western in 1939, sitting in the first row of the Princess Theater in Luling, Texas. I liked the slim young cowboy who rode like the wind on a beautiful palomino and who dispatched the bad guys with authority and style. On the other hand, at that time, my favorite Saturday matinee cowboy was Gene Autry. My loyalty to Gene lasted until he went off to war in 1942, and Republic Pictures boosted Roy Rogers into the studio's top western spot, labeling him "King of the Cowboys."

Roy and his producers had already gathered a remarkable ensemble cast that included George "Gabby" Hayes, the Sons of the Pioneers, and, of course, Trigger. Roy's unassuming but compelling style, Gabby's rustic humor, and the Pioneers' engaging western tunes appealed to me, so when Gene put on his military uniform and flew off into the "wild blue yonder," I easily made the switch.

Within a year, Dale Evans joined Rogers and his buddies and added a dimension to the films that made them special among the genre. My attachment to Roy, Dale, and their friends continued through the 1940s but was limited to their movie star roles. I knew little about Roy and Dale as recording artists, radio stars, or comic book characters. I just knew that I liked them on the silver screen and the way they enhanced my fantasy world.

In the late 1940s and early 1950s, as I moved into the later teen years, my interest in B Westerns waned, and girls, football, track, and automobiles became more inviting. Not having access to television in my college years, I was unaware that Roy Rogers and Dale Evans were gaining a whole new generation of fans. Indeed, I lost track of my childhood heroes as I concentrated on college, marriage, graduate study, and professional work as a college history teacher. At the same time, when I caught Roy on a television talk show, I always stopped what I was doing to watch and remember.

In the late 1970s, I initiated a course at Ball State University on the history and cultural significance of the B Western. That teaching experience, plus my effort to present academic papers at professional conferences on Roy and Dale, led me to write a book on the professional careers of the couple. The project absorbed my life and that of my family for eighteen years and flooded my mind with the details of their lives. Indeed it permitted me to appreciate the couple from a perspective other than that of a front-row kid. That perspective reveals the couple as cultural icons who achieved fame and significance through long careers of hard work in every aspect of the American entertainment business. Moreover, they carefully controlled and marketed their images while incorporating their Christian faith and family values into their public performances.

I briefly met Roy and Dale twice, only to shake their hands and thank them for being accessible to their fans. In recent years, I have come to know members of the Rogers family, who, in turn, have been generous and warm. I was particularly touched when Dodie Rogers-Patterson paid special attention to my two granddaughters, Taylor and Megan, developing a friendship that influenced them greatly.

As a child, I admired and prized Roy Rogers as a movie hero. Today, he remains so, but I understand him in a broader context, one that reveals him as a cultural icon, who with all of his professional accomplishments, influenced the lives of millions and shaped the idea of the romantic American West.

Raymond E. White, award-winning author of *King of the Cowboys, Queen of the West: Roy Rogers and Dale Evans*

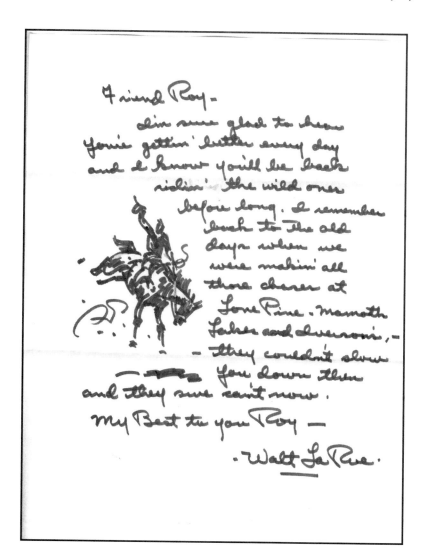

Friend Roy,

I'm sure glad to hear you're getting' better every day, and I know you'll be back ridin' the wild ones before long. I remember back to the old days when we were makin' all those chases at Lone Pine, Mammoth Lakes, and Iverson's—they couldn't slow you down then, and they sure can't now. My best to you, Roy –
Walt LaRue

Walt LaRue (second from left) in a scene with Roy Rogers
"The Cowboy and the Senorita"
- photo provided by the Estate of Walt LaRue

Gabby Hayes and Walt LaRue
- photo provided by the Estate of Walt LaRue

We lost my stepfather, Walt LaRue, in 2010. He was a rodeo champion who turned Hollywood actor and stuntman during the glory days of the B westerns. He was also a guitarist and cowboy-song-loving singer. But he may best be known as a renowned western sketch artist who could create western scenes at the drop of a hat. Today, no western art connoisseur's collection is complete without a Walt LaRue work. Walt loved working with Roy Rogers and Roy's sidekick, Gabby Hayes, as he often worked as Gabby's double. He had Gabby's looks and mannerisms down to a fine art! Like Roy, Walt was a magnetic friend who was generous of heart and as quick with a fun story as Roy Rogers and Gene Autry were with their six-guns. Cowboy heroes needed stuntmen, and Walt never let them down.

John Wilson, stepson of Walt LaRue

to – Roy

You've always been a special person to me. All the Saturday afternoons my brother and I sat and watched you on the screen will always be a special part of my memories. I had so many beautiful pictures of you and your family from magazines and comics, and as young people do, before you married Dale Evans, I was sure you were waiting for me! I am so sorry I tore up my wonderful collection of pictures, but I admit that I resented Dale for many years, although I never stopped loving *you*. I know there were lots of us who felt the same way, and we all still love you for the kind of wonderful person you are, but now we all love and admire Dale, too! That's what happens when you grow up. You get smarter! Take care, dear friend, and feel the love that I send to you both. God bless and thank you!

Bonnie Koehler, Hillsboro, OR - 11/13/90

to – Dale

Just a note to let you know how much I enjoyed your museum on my visit on February 19, 1999. My wife and I both thought the way it was presented was so nice and informative. Over the years I've been a big fan of Roy and yourself. I remember one time when I took my family to the Indiana State Fair just to see your show. On the morning before your show we were eating breakfast at the hotel, and you and Roy came in to have breakfast at the same time. You sat next to us, and it was such a thrill for us and our son. I was aware that Roy was a Mason and a Shriner, and a 33° Mason. I'm also a 33° Mason, and this means a lot to me. I'm sure this was very important to Roy, too, and you could display Roy's Masonic memorabilia in the museum. It would surely be of interest to the public. Thank you, and the very best to you and your family.

Alfred and Elaine Plew, Decatur, IN - 2/28/99

Dale Evans
- photo provided by the Rogers Family

to – Dale

A few weeks ago I was in the depths of depression. I always leave my TV on. That particular day I was kneeling in the hallway crying when I heard your voice from the TV in the bedroom. I ran to see your program. There are so many programs on TBN which minister life, but none is more special to my heart than yours. I was born in 1949 and saw you and Roy at one of the Kentucky state fairs in the late 50s or early 60s. I shall never forget seeing you all in the flesh. You all seem as special to me as my own mom and dad, and they're the tops. I was so grieved to lose Roy. Those smiling eyes certainly are missed. Thank you for caring enough for those of us who love you so dearly to keep on keeping on. You are beautiful!

Ruth Somers, Paducah, KY - 11/21/98

to – Roy

Roy, I live in Splendora, Texas. It's a small town with one school, one store, a post office and a police station. It has a small washerteria, a few stop-and-go's and three filling stations. It is nice here, and it has no beer selling or dance halls. I've been here since I moved from Houston in 1974. When I was young my mom and dad would take us to the old Texan Theaters so we could enjoy Roy over and over. Every Saturday we marched home to "Happy Trails to You" then played with Roy Rogers and Dale Evans paper dolls. I had an old car like Nellybelle, except it was a car instead of a Jeep, and it gave me a run for my money keeping it going. It never failed to get me where I needed to go. It was getting back home that I had to worry about. Poor Pat Brady, I know just how he felt! And Gabby—it was always a joy to hear his drawl of "Well, now, Roy..." Frog was a hit with all the boys, and they all tried to sound just like him. The excitement and joy of the lives you and Dale filled has been much more than what you'd ever think possible, and Dale's book about the loss of your Robin was a great lesson to me as a mother. God bless and keep you, and when God calls me home, I hope I get to meet you.

Ann Cotie, Cleveland, TX - 10/8/96

to – Roy

Lots of folks say things are as American as "baseball, hot dogs and apple pie." I think *nothing* is more wonderfully American than "Roy Rogers and Dale Evans!" This ole baby boomer still has many fond memories of her Saturday afternoons with you at the "picture show." What a hero you were on screen, and what a bigger hero you are in real life. Thanks! I think you're the greatest! "Roy and Dale" are a part of who I am."

Suzy Smith, Rock Spring, GA - 9/30/96

Back in 1994 I was interviewed on BBC Radio about Roy and how I had become the owner of one of his Nathan Turk western shirts, worn by him in a movie. Live, on air, I was surprised to find myself talking to Roy himself. He was calling from Victorville, California. At that time he left an invitation for me to come and visit, and the following year I went to the USA.

Roy was recovering from heart surgery, and a private meeting was set up for me by his son, Dusty. I had a very special time with Roy who sang, yodeled and shared personal memories with me about his family and his movies. He was the perfect gentleman and signed photographs for me. I asked him about my Turk shirt and learned that he used to, on occasion, donate shirts to be auctioned off for charity, especially children's charities. The auction catalog stated that the shirt I acquired was "reputedly made for Roy Rogers in the 1946 Armand Schaeffer/Republic film, 'My Pal Trigger'."

Roy did a tour of England and Scotland, and this is, Dusty believes, how the shirt came to be in Britain. It was a privilege to spend that special time with him, and I really appreciated his kindness all the more because of his health circumstances. Dale was unfortunately away on business, but she later wrote a letter of thanks to me for a Scottish video I had sent to her and Roy. In her note Dale mentions their Scottish daughter, Marion Fleming, known as "Mimi." While on tour here, they met her in an Edinburgh orphanage where she sang to them. They fell in love and brought her to America. I wished I had been able to meet Mimi on my trip, but there was so little time. Roy's kindness that day will always be a treasured memory in my heart."

Tom Sim, Peterhead, Aberdeenshire, Scotland - 8/6/11

Roy Rogers Autographed Photo to Tom Sim

Tom Sim wearing Roy's personal movie shirt
- photos and letter provided by Tom Sim

Letter of thanks from Dale to Tom Sim

to – Dale

 THEN (10/26/98): I wanted to send you the enclosed music box for your birthday. I'm a lifelong fan of you and Roy. I've been to Apple Valley and Victorville many times, starting in the late 1960s. The last time I was there was 4 years ago, and you were celebrating your birthday, and Roy's, too, at Jilly's. I happened to be eating there at the same time and received a piece of birthday cake, along with everyone else in the restaurant. I'm so sorry I was not able to get to Apple Valley in July for Roy's service, but my thoughts and prayers are always with you.

1952   1954   1969
Diana McInerney with Roy Rogers and Dale Evans
- photos provided by Diana McInerney

 NOW (8/12/11): I have been an avid fan of Roy and Dale since I was about 8 years old. I saw them perform many times, starting with Madison Square Garden in the 1950s. I used to go to Apple Valley and Victorville almost every year in the late 1960s and all through the 1970s. Last year I went to the Roy Rogers Museum auction in New York. I thought I would get something, but everything went for so much over the estimate. Also, there was a certain outfit of Dale's that I wanted which was not in the auction, the one she was wearing when I met her at Madison Square Garden in 1954. So many fans loved Roy and Dale, and like me, everyone wanted a piece of their legacy. But we all have their legacy in our hearts.
Diana McInerney, Meriden, CT

to – Roy

You are one of my biggest cowboy heroes, and collecting Roy Rogers memorabilia is a source of great pleasure. I am a retired Navy veteran who is forever your fan.

Robert Kane, Middletown, PA - 10/4/96

Roy Rogers Arcade Cards – photos provided by Robert Kane

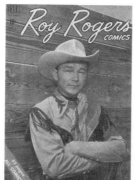

Roy Rogers Trading Cards – photos provided by Robert Kane

Roy Rogers and Bullet – autographed photo provided by Robert Kane

Essay

I grew up watching Roy and Dale on TV, and through the years, their influence stuck with me. The dog featured in my 1998 Christmas card is Bullet Junior. He was the first dog I had as an adult, and he was born January 1, 1995, the day after Roy and Dale's anniversary. If I announced, *"Roy's wonder dog, Bullet!"* (as in the beginning of the Roy Rogers Show on TV) my Bullet would come running.

Although I've always had Roy and Dale in my mind and heart, my thoughts of them renewed when, as an adult, I adopted my third child, a daughter, Gemma, who was born in the Philippines and came home to me in Indiana in 1990. Roy and Dale's open hearts about adoption were inspiring to generations of young adults. That was also about the time I became a lifetime member of the Roy Rogers Riders Club.

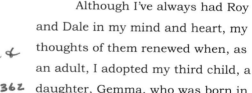

My birthday is the same as Dale's, October 31, and my granddaughter, Loran, was born October 20, 2005, the same day as Mindy's granddaughter. And yes, I do drive a Jeep named Nellybelle. One of these days, when I retire, I plan to paint a mural on my garage door similar to the final scene of the Roy Rogers TV shows. I also began a Bible Study based on the Roy Rogers Show TV series.

Roy and Dale left a legacy that can't be forgotten.
Katrina Harder, Nashville, IN - 9/14/11

to – Roy

I'm enclosing a picture of my husband as a boy and would love it if you would autograph the snapshot. My husband went to see you in Chicago either in '48 or '49, he can't remember exactly what year it was, but he has never forgotten the rodeo or tapping Trigger on the rump as you came around the ring shaking everyone's hand. He's had a program from that particular rodeo for years, but somehow it's been misplaced, and I'm afraid I'm at fault. At times I put things away and forget where I put them. Ron let me know if I find it we'd take the first plane to California to see you. He wanted to show you the program, and I believe go back in time to where a ten-year-old boy went to a rodeo in Chicago and met his idol, Roy Rogers, King of the Cowboys. He'll never forget how you got upset with the ushers because there were stopping the youngsters from coming down to the edge so they could shake your hand, so much so that you got on the loud speaker to say, "I came to see the kids!" Then you rode around standing on Triggers back so you could reach up to shake even more hands. You were Ron's hero, and now, at 52 years of age, he still places you as should be—high on a pedestal as the King of the Cowboys!

Janice and Ron Kornas, Streator, IL - 11/12/90

Young Ron Kornas sharing the couch with his hero, Roy Rogers
- autographed photo provided by Ron Kornas

My Grandma Christian, Our Father in Heaven, and Roy and Dale provided me with the most influence and guidance throughout my lifetime. It was my Grandma Christian whose influence early on in my life helped to steer my direction in life toward the Lord and these two special and unique individuals known as Roy and Dale.

My Grandma's last name was Christian, but she was a "Christian" in the truest form. She encouraged me to get to know, love and admire Roy and Dale for who they really were. She insisted that I learn all I could of my heroes and their lives outside the movies and television. *"That's what you need to do for yourself, and you will know if these two special individuals are worthy of your admiration."*

When Dale's first book, "Angel Unaware," came out in 1953, my grandma bought it for me and my older sister to share. I read that book at age 8 for the first time. I love it, have read it many times, and still have that very book.

Like millions of other little buckaroos, I wanted to be adopted by Roy and Dale and live the cowgirl way of life. As I grew into a young lady, Roy and Dale never left my heart or my soul. Every time I had a decision to make, small or large, I always asked myself, "What would Roy and Dale suggest I do?" After I married and had my children, I told them many of the very same things my Grandma Christian once told me, and I often used Roy and Dale as examples in situations that arose throughout my children's growing years.

In the fall of 1998, there was a festival held in Branson, MO called "Cowboys, Heroes & Friends." I had to work all weekend and couldn't attend. Several western stars were going to be present, including Dale Evans. Gee, it had been only a few months since Roy had graduated into Heaven. Bless Dale's heart for wanting to attend!

The "Cowboys, Heroes & Friends" festival had their 1998 awards ceremony at the Dixie Stampede Dinner & Show, where my oldest son, Larry, still performs as trick rider in the show. Larry had the honor and pleasure of showing Dale around the backstage area. After posing for pictures, Dale asked the performers if any of them really knew who Roy Rogers and Dale Evans were. My son answered, "Oh, my goodness yes! My mom told my brother, sister and myself all about Roy Rogers and Dale Evans, and how you two have been an inspiration to her and influenced her life. Mom used you as fine examples to pattern our lives by." Dale replied back with, "Well, good for your Mama!"

When the "Cowboys, Heroes & Friends" festival returned to Branson in 1999, I was so excited to attend with my new husband, Jim. We had met two years earlier when I thought I was content with my life, which included my three beautiful children—daughter Chantelle, and sons, Larry and Kris, as well as a fine son-in-law, Mike, and my two "pet children"—a tabby cat, Mr. Clarence Garfield, and my Chihuahua, Miss Felina Marie. I wasn't looking for a new husband. But then I met a man named Jim who wasn't looking for a wife, and soon we both realized we were simply meant to be. The trip to the festival was a gift from my new husband. I was going to meet Dale!

When we arrived in Branson, we heard that Dale had cancelled because her doctor said she shouldn't fly with her new pacemaker. Oh, how sad I felt. The last day of the festival happened to be Dale's birthday. Dale Warren, the then "straw boss" of the Sons of the Pioneers called and got Dale on the phone. When she answered, the crowd roared. She asked, "What in the world is going on?" Mr. Warren told her that the crowd in Branson had something to tell her. That's when everyone sang "Happy Birthday" to her via the telephone. After we finished, you could hear Dale sniffling with emotion, and she told us to please hold on while she blew her nose. Oh what a thrill it was for me to be there and be able to communicate in such a way with Dale, even if only via a telephone!

After purchasing a computer in 2001, the door to the world seemed to open for me. When I got online for the first time, I immediately typed "Roy Rogers and Dale Evans," and that moment changed my life. Jim and I learned there was an annual festival in Roy's honor held near his childhood home of Duck Run, OH. Via the Internet, we met and became friends with another fan, Shirley Duke. In 2002, the three of us journeyed to Portsmouth, OH and attended the Roy Rogers Festival together. That's where Jim and I met Cheryl

Rogers-Barnett and her husband, Larry, for the first time. That festival was the beginning of many fun-filled adventures at western events along the trail.

But it was in February of 2003 when Jim, Shirley and I fulfilled my childhood dream. There I was, finally standing in front of the Roy Rogers and Dale Evans museum in California, taking it all in, gazing up at the large statue of Trigger and at the fort-like building that housed my heroes' collections and belongings, and I just got down and my knees, kissed the ground and thanked God for allowing me to get there before I passed this world. I cried like a baby.

After the museum closed for the day, we headed for Sunset Hills Memorial Park. I couldn't believe how serene and peaceful it was, and I fully understood why Roy and Dale had chosen this place, nestled at the base of a mountain, near where they used to ride the trails on Trigger and Buttermilk, for their final resting place. We placed flowers on their graves and sat for a long while as I "talked" with my heroes, Roy and Dale.

Later that trip we attended the western festival, and since that 2003 gathering in California, the "Duke Gang" as we call ourselves, has taken many a trip together to honor Roy and Dale.

Jim and I live close to Branson, and we video-catalogued the ten-month construction period of the new Roy Rogers and Dale Evans Museum there. When the groundbreaking ceremony took place, Jim and I took our own shovel just in case we were allowed to shovel a little dirt for the new museum in Roy and Dale's honor. It was a blessing and an honor to do so along side Dusty.

On February 11, 2005, the Lord took my mom on home. Two days later, as we left the funeral home after making arrangements, Jim asked me where I wanted to go. I asked, "Would you please take me to the museum? I feel the need to be close to Roy and Dale today. I just have to go there." Later, I knew it was exactly where I needed to be.

I'm now a senior, and my birthday is November 4th, one day before Roy's. My daughter's birthday is October 30th, one day before Dale's. That's significant to us.

For the past few years, Jim and I have had the honor of being on the Roy Rogers Festival committee in Portsmouth, OH. I love it! For Roy fans, it's a family reunion.

.

.

.

.

.

.

.

.

.

.

.

.

.

.

.

.

.

.

.

.

.

.

.

.

.

.

.

.

.

.

.

.

.

.

.

.

.

.

.

.

.

.

.

.

.

.

.

.

.

.

.

.

.

.

.

.

.

.

.

.
.

.

.

.

.

.

.

.

.

.

.

.

.

.

.

.

.

.

.

.

.

.

.

.

.

.

.

.

.

.

.

.

.

.

.

.

.

.

.

.

.

.

.

.

.

.

.

.

.

.

.

.

.

.

.

.

.

.

.

.

.

.

.

.

.

.

.

.

.

.
.

.

.

.

.

.

.

.

.

.

.

.

.

.

.

.

.

.

.

.

.

.

.

.

.

.

.

.

.

.

.

.

.

.

.

.

.

.

.

.

.

.

.

.

.

.

.

.

.

.

.

.

.

.

.

.

.

.

.

.

.

.

.

.

.

.

.

.

.

.

.

.

.

.

.

.
.

.

.

.

.

.

.

.

.

.

.

.

.

.

.

.

.

.

.

.

.

.

.

.

.

.

.

.

.

.

.

.

.

.

.

.

.

.

.

.

.

.

.

.

.

.

.

.

.

.

.

.

.

.

.

.

.

.

.

.

.

.

.

.

.

.

.

.

.

.

.

.

.

.

.

.
..

..

..

..

..

..

..

..

..

..

..

..

..

..

..

..

..

..

..

..Roy Rogers and Dale Evans will always be my heroes. Their family values and love of God, family and country, reign forever in my heart.
Carolyn and Jim Van Horn, aka Buffalo Gal and Buffalo Jim - 9/3/11

Buffalo Jim (Jim Van Horn) and Buffalo Gal (Carolyn Van Horn) with Miss Felina Marie - photo provided by Carolyn Van Horn

176

---

to – Dale

I promised my mother that when I grew up I would either marry my dad or Roy Rogers! Thank you, Dale Evans, for sharing your wonderful husband with all of us for so many, many years. Thanks for being the perfect life mate for him. You are a lovely star, Mrs. Slye. It has been my good fortune to have lived in such a time as to share my time with you. I may have thought I wanted to grow up and marry Roy Rogers, but I always thought you looked like my mom. Much love, good health and sincere good wishes!

Jennie Brooks, Continental Divide, NM - 10/21/98

---

to – Roy and Dale

I so remember the great movies you made. We lived 15 miles away, but came to Napanee on Saturday, and us kids got to go to the movies for 15 cents each. The rest of the time we played cowboys when not attending our one-room school that was on our farm. I'm right now looking at one of your books that my brother gave me for my 11th birthday in 1948, *Roy Rogers and the Deadly Treasure.* It cost him the princely sum of 25 cents at that time. I also got a glossy 8x10 photo of Roy and Trigger free for taking a Quaker Rolled Oats box top to our Granada Theatre. What great treats the book and the photo are. I just had to drop you a line and tell you that we have loved you both for years and that you are in our prayers. With all our love and well wishes,

Verna and Jack Morgan, Napanee, Ontario, Canada - 10/8/96

---

to – Roy

I saw you and Dale and Trigger at the American Royal in Kansas City. I think you said you were 65 then. It was wonderful. My wife, Kay, and I showed horses for about 30 years and still trail ride a lot. We love you both. My wife has promised me that they will play "Happy Trails" at my funeral. I couldn't wish for anything better.

Paul Simpson, Iola, KS - 11/4/96

---

to – Dale

I am so sorry for the loss of Mr. Rogers. I apologize for the lateness of this note, but I have found it extremely difficult to write this. I've started a dozen or more times, but I either don't know what to say, or my emotions take over and I just can't continue. It's time though. Where do I begin? I can't imagine my life without Mr. Rogers and Ms. Evans having been a part of it. My fondest memories of my own dad were of the two of us sitting on Saturday mornings and watching the Roy Rogers Show together. My five brothers and sisters are all fans as well. How privileged I feel that Roy was a part of my childhood, and continues to be a part of me now. He was a very special person, as are you.. It seems you truly live the "code of the west," a rare thing these days. As special as Roy was to us, I can only imagine the sense of loss you feel. Though I feel as though I've lost a little piece of me that he touched, I cling tighter to that piece of my heart, and take it with me wherever I go. I think of him and can hear him singing with the Sons of the Pioneers or see him proudly atop Trigger with Bullet by their side, and my heart smiles. What wonderful memories. I know now that he is once again atop Trigger at the Double R Bar, working the ranch with his old friends, Gabby, Pat, Buttermilk, Bullet and Trigger, Jr. Again, I remember him with a smile, as I hope all of you can now. I'm sure he would like that! I was fortunate enough to have seen you both at a Golden Boot Awards some years ago. It was the thrill of my life. And so often...I thank God...for Roy Rogers and Dale Evans...and all they stand for. And Dusty, if you read this, keep singing. We'd love to hear more songs from you! Your dad would love it, too.

Michelle Tenney, Glyndon, MD - undated

Essay

Long ago I met Roy at a Western Music Association event, just as he was leaving. There were two big State Troopers keeping everyone from getting too close to Roy, but they let me stand between them because I was so short. Doing so put me right in front. When Roy looked at the Troopers, there I was, and with a smile that would light up the world, he just put out his hand and took mine. Wow.

Years later I met Dale at the Festival of the West. She was in the tent having lunch, sitting all alone. My husband, John, and I grabbed a sandwich, sat down by her, and introduced ourselves. She was so friendly and so happy to not be sitting alone anymore. It was an amazing, cherished encounter.

One of my most prized possessions is a framed photo of Roy and Dale along with a 1984 "allowance" check made out to Mrs. Roy Rogers, signed by Roy, and endorsed and cashed by Dale. I so enjoy just looking at that small piece of history and remembering all the good those two people brought to this world. Roy and Dale were wonderful people through and through.

Janet McBride, Yodeling Queen, Western Music Hall of Fame Artist, Academy of Western Artists Yodeler of the Year, Gene Autry Museum Lifetime Achievement Award winner, yodeling mentor to country music star LeeAnn Rimes, and Author of *The Janet McBride Life Story: Still Lovin' the Ride*

Janet McBride's 7th CD:
"Still Loving The Ride"
- CD cover provided by Janet McBride

Janet McBride, Dale Evans and Janet's husband John Ingram at the Festival of the West
- photo provided by Janet McBride

1984 "Allowance" check to Dale from Roy
- photo provided by Janet McBride

to – Roy

THEN (10/18/96): I'm 67 years old and you were my hero from the start. June 11, 1953 I had a baby girl and named her Robin after your very own little angel. I love to ride, and I volunteer at the Rialto Theater in Joliet, IL. Many, many stars have performed here. Built in 1926 it is now on the Historical List. It would be my dream to see you here, and I've already told them I'm not working if Roy comes. I'll be front row center for sure!

NOW (6/14/11): The 40's were my high school days. At age 13 my parents bought me real cowboy boots in Colorado, and I have them yet today. In no time at all I hand embroidered and sewed my own cowboy shirt, and I had horse statues all over my bedroom. Three years after my daughter, Robin, was born, in July of 1956, we had a son, Kevin Michael. Sadly, like Roy and Dale, I lost my Robin far too early.

At the age of twelve I began drawing movie stars from their pictures and sending the drawings to them. To my, and my parents' surprise, they would send back autographed pictures and comment on my drawings. The 1942 letter I'm enclosing came from Roy's secretary, and later, when I saw Roy in Chicago, I took the letter backstage and he personally signed it for me.
Jo Anne (Ford) Mackay, Joliet, IL

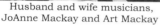

Husband and wife musicians,
JoAnne Mackay and Art Mackay

1943 - Dale Evans and Roy Rogers at the airport

- photos provided by JoAnne Mackay

1942 letter to JoAnne Mackay

Collage of a young JoAnne Mackay and photos
of her children, Kevin, and look-alike daughter, Robin

A page from JoAnne Mackay's "Roy Rogers" scrapbook
- all photos provided by JoAnne Mackay

to – Roy

You have always been the one that I have looked up to, trying to do what is always right, even though it would sometimes be almost impossible to do. Somehow I have accomplished a lot of pride trying to copy your way of cowboy dreams. You are the best example of what any man could ever accomplish on this earth. I was born 10/7/33, as a tenant farmer's son. I would see your movies on Saturdays whenever we could make it to town—if we could get enough gas to get to town, and if the roads were passable. Most of the times we would have to go by wagon or horse so we had plenty of practice riding horses at an early stage. It seems like that will never leave us because I would rather ride down the trails more than any other thing. I had my own horse in my early years while on the farm—could not afford a saddle so you know how I learned to ride. After my you-know-what got sore, I got a blanket, then later, as times got a little better, I got a second-hand saddle. The high time was when my dad bought me a second-hand pair of chaps, child size 12, and they had Texas Centennial stenciled on each leg. Boy was I the stuff. I thought I was Roy Rogers—had a hat, spurs, chaps, and I would saddle up and ride off into the sunset, and I was really *in* your movies and trying some of your tricks. I guess I would have been about 8 years old at that time. My Roy Rogers dream has always been in the back of my mind, so in 1983 I said if there was ever a time I could have my dream come true, it would be now. I bought an old Ranch King saddle, and finally found my "Trigger." In 1992 my horse got sick and the vet said she only had a short time to live. I had to put her down and buried her in a grave and put flowers on it, and that was about the worst time for me, and I still have not adjusted. There will never be another horse like this, so I can relate to you and Trigger. I am sort of lost without my horse, but life goes on. Pardner, I want you to know what an influence you've had on my life, and I will never forget you and Dale. I admire both of you for what you have done for us all.

Joe Hluchanek, Columbus, TX - 9/29/96

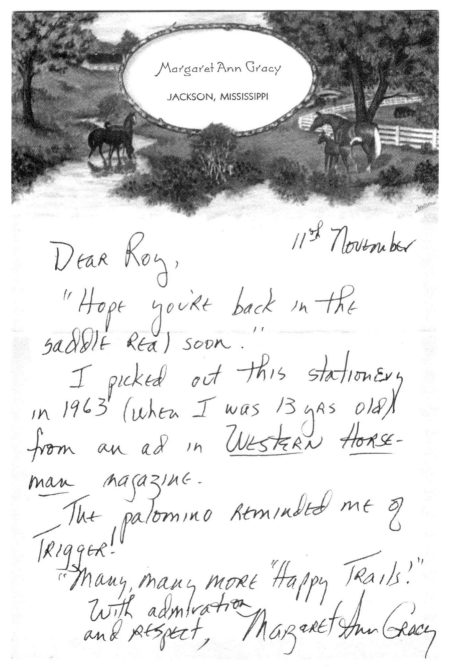

Margaret Ann Gracy

JACKSON, MISSISSIPPI

11ᵗʰ November

Dear Roy,

"Hope you're back in the saddle real soon."

I picked out this stationery in 1963 (when I was 13 yrs old) from an ad in UESTERN Horseman magazine.

The palomino reminded me of TRIGGER!

"Many, many more "Happy Trails!"

With admiration and respect, Margaret Ann Gracy

letter from Margaret Ann Gracy on 1963 stationery
- letter provided by Margaret Ann Gracy

to – Roy

My dad always said that he used to sell you the Buick automobiles that you used to ride in the Santa Claus Day Parade. He used to work at Phil Hall Buick on Sunset Blvd in Hollywood. The last parade I remember seeing was on Sunset Blvd, right in front of Phil Hall Buick. All the other parades used to be on Hollywood Blvd. When we were young we were always told that we came from the same orphanage some of your kids were from. We drove out to your ranch once, but had to stay in the car while our mom went inside. I'm 48 years old and I used to be in love with you as a little girl, until I found out your real wife was Dale. I don't know if you remember my adopted dad, but he was a swell guy. He used to have racehorses. Every time I used to take my 2 sons to Disneyland from Vegas, we used to stop by your museum. We always wanted to run into you, but never did. Still, you will always be in my heart.
Judy Metz, Las Vegas, NV - 11/2/90

to – Dale

Please forgive my delay in sending sincere sympathy for Roy's passing. It was difficult at the time to put my shock and sorrow into words, and today seems no easier. Please know that you and your family are in my prayers. I am of the generation that grew up with you. My lunch bucket had "Roy and Dale" on the cover and was a cherished article. As all the little girls of my time, I wore pigtails and western wear when possible.

Diane Waddell in her cowgirl pigtails
-photo provided by Diane Waddell

Thank you for the treasured childhood memories. Twelve years ago I lost my dad to a heart attack, and I understand the emptiness your children are experiencing. Knowing my dad is with Jesus softens the hurt. However, he is always with me in my heart. I thank God for a wonderful father and for happy memories. May your children experience the warmth of fond memories as well. May God bless you and your family during this first Christmas without Roy.
Diane Waddell, Rocklin, CA -12/21/98

From my earliest memories, music was there—all kinds of music, gospel, classical, big band, bluegrass, and of course, western. My father would wake us up on Saturday mornings playing and yodeling along with his Sons of the Pioneers albums, opening my bedroom door with '*Cool...clear...water, water, water...*' pouring from his mouth.

I am a child of the fifties. Unfortunately for me, it was the late fifties, and so my concept of Roy and Dale Rogers was formed from what I saw Saturday mornings on TV. His movies always caught my attention because those guys would be singing the songs my dad sang. So, being the romantic that I am, I fell in love with the handsome cowboy on TV who was so much like my dad. My dad *was* Roy Rogers to me. He was raised in a ranching family in central Texas, and music was a big part of his upbringing. My Grandpa led the singing and my Granny played the old upright (always slightly out of tune) piano at Elm Grove Baptist Church. My mom was like Dale. She sang, she had spunk and sass, and she made my dad smile. I would sit in the front pew of church as a child and listen to my parents sing duets with their beautiful, harmonious voices. And at home, my mom played the piano and we sang and sang. I felt like I lived with a slightly younger version of Roy Rogers and Dale Evans.

My parents' faith was the whole premise of their lives, as it was for Roy and Dale. When I was young, I read Dale's book, *Angel Unaware*, and wondered if I would have the courage to raise a Down's syndrome child, then face the loss of that child with such strength. As I watched my mother faithfully face countless surgeries due to an accident when I was nine, and the years of health problems, the Lord taught me that He is faithful through the good times and bad times of life.

And so it is for me as it is for so many. Roy Rogers and Dale Evans are a part of me. I ooze western. Several years ago I was thinking about why I had such a passion for all things from the West, and my mom thought maybe I was looking for a simpler way of life. However, my search for a simpler life has led me to be an avid collector of all things western and Native American, which isn't so simple sometimes (or cheap either.) When I saw an ad from a company that had sent a representative to the Rogers' estate sale and purchased some of their Navajo weavings, I had to own one. It is slightly beat up, but I was told that "Roy liked it that way and didn't want it repaired." So I have a small Germantown weaving that someone wore a hole through the middle of, and every time I look at it, I hear music."

Debbie Font -10/1/03

Debbie and Kathy and their "no-they-don't-do-tricks-like-Trigger" horses
- photo provided by Debbie Font

---

to – Roy

My name is João Alberto, and I am a Portuguese journalist, 37 years old. Since I was a child I've read a lot of your great adventures in many comics and magazines. I still do so nowadays, and I've seen a lot of your movies, too. Roy Rogers is much better than Batman! I send you all my best wishes!

João Alberto, Portugal - 12/26/90

---

to – Roy

THEN (10/7/96): I think you and my dad had something in common. In the late 40s and early 50s he was the trainer for Frank Egner who owned the Mill Stream Stables in Findley, Ohio where they had a yellow stud called "Phillips 66". From the stories I've been told, this horse was the sire of your second Trigger. Phillips 66 was also the sire of "Millstream Hub", a horse Dad showed all over the country. In my tack room I have pictures of many cowboy stars. One of the pictures of you, Roy, is where you are sitting at a table with a box of Wheaties and a glass milk bottle, the ones that had the cardboard tops. I am proud to have watched you at the movies, proud to have seen your TV shows, and very proud to say I never forgot the difference between right and wrong that you taught me with every show we watched.

NOW (6/14/11):

"Twilight Time in a Cowboy's Eyes" by John Stukins

When I watched my dad pull himself up on a horse in his later years,
As I would spring up on my horse with ease,
I would think, "Looks like it's twilight time for him."

Over the years I watched so many as they would try so hard
Showing or trail riding their horses, and I would say to myself,
"Looks like twilight time is catching up with them."

I guess over the years I just didn't notice things were getting harder to do.
Seems like the horses were getting taller, the ground getting harder.
"Can it be?" I say to myself, "No way. It's not yet twilight time for me."

But you know something I saw today?
There's grass starting to grow in my round pen.
Always before it had been dirt churned by the many colts and horses I worked
And broke in that ole round pen year after year.

I walked on into the house and laid down on the couch,
Something I have been doing a lot more of this past year.
As I lay there thinking about all the good horses I rode for people in the past,
The 45 years I have been training horses,
I say to myself...damn, John, looks like it's twilight time."

John Stukins, Avinger, TX

to – Roy

      This is a letter from your number-one fan. You were my first boyfriend. I compared every boy and every man from my "pre-teen and up" years to you. I was madly, desperately in love with you! I was born in Mexico City, Mexico. My parents were born in the USA. My father was in export for Eastman Kodak then became a VIP with the movie studios. He was also a "go-between" between the Mexican movies and the US movies, stars and producers. I went to many a movie set with my father. Much fun! In the 40s and 50s in Mexico we did not have all the media down there. Everyone knew I adored you, so everyone brought me records, photos and stories about Roy Rogers when they came south. I cherished everything. Matter of fact, I used to play your records while I ate until one day I sat on them by mistake. The world seemed to come to an end for me with the loss. Horses were another of my loves. I tried to find and copy your Trigger. No such luck. But I did ride with the Mexican Jumping Olympic Team. I had a bad fall and my jumping days were over. So I picked up my dressage and continued on and now teach and train dressage in Orange County, CA. In 1954 I met a tall, handsome man from Ohio (Youngstown.) He had blue eyes and brown hair. He didn't wear cowboy boots, but rather a Naval Officer's uniform. But you were still my first love. As a young girl your looks and your voice took my breath away. But as I grew older and smarter, your character on screen and off became more important to me. When you married Dale, I hated her. I cried and cried! Since then I have continued to buy whatever I could with or about Roy Rogers. The world needs men like you, and every girl should have you to love and to look up to. There is no one in the world like you. Please say hello to your lovely wife, Dale, (whom I have forgiven for marrying you!) your especially nice son, Dusty, and please rub Trigger's nose for me. From a redhead who would do anything for you, con todo mi amor [with all my love].

Mary Kay Gillen, Yorba Linda, CA - 10/5/96

to – Roy

As a young boy in the 1940s and early 1950s I read everything I could about you and considered you to be the second most important person in the world (after my mother and father.) You and your support members in the movies and comics were always true to the right cause, eager to correct the wrongs of society. One of the first things that drew you close was that we had the same first initials of our first and last names. After these many years, I still think of you when I sign my initials to a memo or other document. The manner in which you treated Trigger also made a strong impression on me, one that has lasted to this day. My brother trained in his early years to be a jockey, and my wish was that he ride as safely and carefully as you always did, and that above all, he treat the animals respectfully. My very best wishes are extended across the miles to both you and Dale.

Ronald Rindelhardt, Lyndon Center, VT - 11/12/90

to – Roy

When I was a teen I had three pictures on my wall of my heros—you, Van Johnson and Franchot Tone—now that's quite a threesome, huh? I'm now going on 58 and still consider you my hero. My heart was broken when you married Dale, but after all these years I'm so proud you did. You have both been so inspirational throughout the years. You marriage, your adoptions, your causes and your high moral standards have been of the highest quality, and even the tabloids can find no cause to write "sensational" bad things about either of you, only good. That's so rare. May God bless both of you and grant you only "Happy Trails.

June Leib, Winchester, IL - 11/17/90

to – Dale

For a long time I've wanted to write to you. The first time I read your book, *Angel Unaware*, I was about 12 years old. I borrowed it from the library at church. The second time I read it was in 1981 after our daughter, Mindy, was born with Down Syndrome. First of all I want to thank you for the book about your beloved Robin and your family. If God would send such a child to Dale and Roy, then surely he was with my husband, Steve, and me also. That fact alone made the early days easier. Thank you for sharing what was in your heart! Nine years after Mindy was born our second daughter arrived. We named her Robin. She is such a sweetheart and so wonderful to her big sister, Mindy. God chose her special for a sister to Mindy, I'm sure. Robin always keeps an eye out for Mindy. She is just the kindest, most understanding little girl! She has learned lessons in life already in her eight years that others don't learn in a lifetime. Steve and I were so sorry to learn of Roy's death. We all lost a hero. I know you miss him terribly, and I'm so sorry. Enclosed is a photo of Mindy and our Robin. Aren't they just the cutest kids? I hope it's a bright spot for you. Once again I thank you for the story of your Robin. It helped me more than you could ever know.

Stephanie Norburg, Albany, IL - 1/13/99

1998 - Robin and Mindy Norburg
- photo provided by Stephanie Norburg

to – Dale

"I hope you enjoy my tributes:

"King of the Cowboys" by Ronnie Duffey

As a child we didn't have many toys,
But our Saturdays were still full of joys,
As we watched on our T.V. Roy Rogers,
"KING OF THE COWBOYS"

We waited for Saturday mornings with glee
As we jumped from our beds to watch T.V.
As we gathered on the floor, a little fast, a little slow
There's one thing we did know,
It wouldn't be long before the Roy Rogers Show.

As we waited for Roy, Dale, Pat Brady or Gabby Hayes,
Trigger, Buttermilk, Bullet and Nellybelle too,
Our excitement ran through and through, for once again we knew
What a joy it would be, to see the King of the Cowboys on our T.V.

Double pearl-handled silver pistols and a scarf around his neck,
Roy would whip those bad buys all the way to heck.
Ridin', ropin', shootin' too, no one could do what Roy could do,
For he is the King of the Cowboys through and through.

With the bad guys no longer on the loose,
Locked up tightly in the calaboose, there was no more
For Roy and Dale to do, then we knew the show was through.
As they climbed upon their horses and headed home under a
Sky of blue, Roy and Dale would sing "Happy Trails to You!"

Many a King may come and man a King may go,
But there's only one King of the Cowboys
And one Roy Rogers Show.
And one day when Roy is laid to rest,
We can surely say he gave us his best,
And safely we then say with many other good things
The King of the Cowboys has gone to meet the King of Kings.

And as Roy rises in a sky of blue,
He'll stop one more time to sing,
"Happy Trails to You"

"Queen of the Cowgirls" by Ronnie Duffey

Of the cowboys on the Silver Screen
Roy Rogers was the King, and though
Many things may go unseen,
We cannot forget his Queen.

As beautiful as a western sunset across a lake,
With her no other cowboy chances would take,
For fear his neck Roy would break.
For her heart was solemnly true, to her faithful companion
Through and through, and everyone on the silver screen,
Knew Dale Evans was Roy's queen.

"QUEEN OF THE COWGIRLS" she will always be as she came on our T.V.
On Saturday mornings as we all know, Roy without his queen
Wouldn't have had a show, for wherever he went she would go,
Helping Roy beat the bad guys from head to toe,
With a rope, a gun, or a frying pan, Dale Evans, Queen of the Cowgirls,
Stood by her man.

Dale Evans was this pretty lady's name, and on the silver screen
And in Roy's heart she won her fame, ropin', ridin', and shootin' straight,
Dale Evans was never late.
By her man she stood like a beam,
While in her eyes such a gleam,
That everybody knew she was Roy's queen.

As the show begun, so would it end,
With both the King and Queen riding side by side
As they would sing a song we all knew,
"Happy Trails to You."

And though the King has left his Queen, it is not too late,
For they have still one more date,
For his Queen at the Pearly Gate, Roy Rogers will wait,
Until together again they will ride side by side
On streets of gold and in Heaven's purest blue, to sing one more time
"Happy Trails to You."

Ronnie Duffey, Pigeon Forge, TN - 12/6/98

Essay

As a child I would spend Saturday mornings sitting in front of the television with my brothers anxiously awaiting their next adventure to unfold. Roy Rogers and Dale Evans held a special place in my heart. My youth gave way to adulthood, and our paths separated. However, many years and miles later I once again found myself on the same trail with those I had ridden with in my childhood. They were still fighting evil forces but had holstered their six-guns and were now doing it as witnesses. I was nice to see that some memories will always remain a warm campfire and a pleasant song.

Happy trails to you, my brother and my sister, until we meet again.

Dwight Hatcher - 10/8/03

---

to – Roy

Oh how the two of you, Dale and you, have warmed our hearts over the years, and I so enjoy seeing Dale on TBN. For you:

> In Indiana when I was a very young lady
> And TV was new to our house
> I'd sit down and turn the dial
> Lots of people appeared on the screen
> Of course there was you
>
> Roy and Trigger across the picture
> Before long you know
> They were part of our family
> Then appeared a lady named Dale
> She became a part of the family, too
>
> I moved out to the West
> Los Angeles to Las Vegas
> And often a drive thru Palmdale
> Off #15 onto Roy Rogers Drive
> Keep lookin' for Trigger, and Roy
> Dressed in his western best."

Heart Shapré, author, singer, songwriter - Hearts and Roses Songs, *Las Vegas, NV - 9/30/96*

---

to – Roy

      I am 51 years old and grew up in Chillicothe, Ohio. We were a very poor family, living on a truck farm outside of town. There were eight children, four girls and four boys, and our father was killed in a motorcycle accident when I was four. Our stepfather died when I was eleven, in 1949, so my mom raised all of us on hard work, dogged honesty, and Roy Rogers as our role model. Although we didn't have money for entertainment, somehow my mom and granddad always managed to get us all to the Majestic Theater in Chillicothe whenever a new Roy Rogers movie was released. At home, in the little fields and creeks near our house, we played "cowboys." When there was disagreement over the proper way a cowboy would handle a situation, we often spoke of writing to you to ask your opinion. You would, of course, have never received the letter, as we were certain that Hollywood was in Texas, as all cowboys were in Texas. I remember when you and Dale were married. I was delighted. My role in our games at home was as Dale Evans. At 14, I tried to decorate all my clothes with beads and fringe to look like you guys. I have followed your lives since then...the ranch and the children, and the benefits you hosted. It has been so good to know that you are always reliably the people we came to know so long ago. And you both stayed so young from living such a beautiful and inspiring life. You have given me and my brothers and sisters so much inspiration, and you have influenced my life more than you may imagine. We care about you, Roy, and our thoughts are always with you.
Dody Engel, Aurora, CO - 11/11/90

---

to – Roy

      As a child I never missed one of your movies. You were my hero then, and that feeling has never been forgotten. I think I made a good choice. You have been a good example to follow. Thank you for the good you have done and the wonderful entertainment you have provided. There will always be a special place in my heart for you.
Gerry Emerick, Turner, MI - 10/1/96

to – *Roy and Dale*

At different times growing up Roy was my boyfriend, friend, father, brother, and mentor, and you, Dale, write words that have meant so much to me. I've loved you both dearly for as long as I can remember. I visited your museum, but missed seeing you. It was over Thanksgiving week, and they told me you were there most weekdays until you had your surgery. I hope I can come back sometime and you will be there. I have a Post Cereal Roy Rogers Double R Bar Ranch, but I didn't see one in your museum. I thought maybe you might like to have one for the museum. If so, I will be very glad to mail it to you. You made my life so special, and I would be so happy to give something special back. I hope you get this letter and my loving Christmas wish. God bless you all.

Christine Pearce, Kingman, KS – 12/90

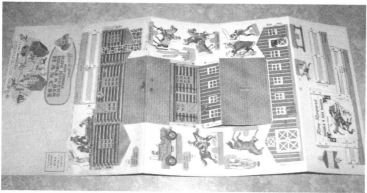

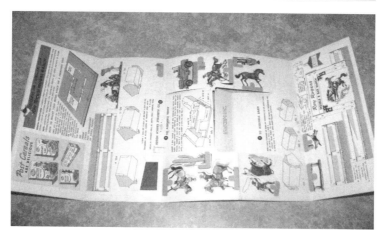

From the Roy Rogers and Dale Evans of Christine Pearce
- six photos provided by Christine Pearce

to – Roy and Dale

I have been a fan for as long as I can remember, and I still love anything I can get my hands on that has to do with Roy Rogers and Dale Evans. In June of 1987 my husband, two daughters and I took a trip to California, and the Roy Rogers Museum was immediately added as a tour stop. When we walked into the museum I couldn't believe my eyes. Roy was standing in the lobby. He had a cast on his left arm, and I was speechless. I told my daughters I was going to ask you if I could have my picture taken with you. My daughters said, "Mom, he'll never agree to that." But I couldn't resist asking anyway. You got the biggest smile on your face and graciously agreed. You put your arm around my shoulder, and I thought I was going to faint. I was so excited. That photo of you, me, and my daughters is one of my most valued possessions. Thank you so much for your generosity. You have both been such an inspiration to young and old alike. You are truly a rare and loving couple, and I am so thankful to have grown up in your era. May God bless you! I know I do.

Joanne Zuber, Norway, IA - 11/12/96

1987 - Joanne Zuber, Roy Rogers, Chris Zuber, Patty Zuber
- photo by Terry Zuber and provided by Joanne Zuber

to – Roy

THEN (10/4/96): Just a note to let you know how much you are admired and loved. When I was a child my parents took the family to see you and your lovely wife, Dale, when you had your hunting dogs in an area just outside of Marysville, California. You stopped your activity and let my father take a picture of you with my sister and me. Just last Christmas my sister had that picture put on a coffee mug for me. I will always treasure it. I have it on display because I don't want it broken, so no one is allowed to use it! I remember running up to Dale Evans to find out where Roy Rogers was so we could see you. She was so sweet, and she put her arm around me and told me the direction she had just seen you. I was so thrilled I told everyone about Dale Evans putting her arm around me, and then Roy Rogers stopped and let us take a picture! All of your fans admire you for your high morals and the clean movies you made. Today I can't even take my grandchildren to see a movie because of sex, violence, and bad language (unless it's a Disney Cartoon.) Thank you! May God bless and keep you.

NOW (7/3/11): Roy and my father, Roy Grider, were good friends. Mr. Rogers would come to Gridley, CA to see my dad. Dad was a city policeman at the time. When the photo you see was taken, my dad helped Roy map out a trail for the dog trials being held that weekend. When Roy and my dad were setting up the trails, my dad rode Trigger and Roy rode Buttermilk. I also have a picture taken at the same time with Roy, my sister, Shirley, and me."
Patsy McComas, Oroville, CA

1951 – Roy Rogers setting the trails for the hunting dog trials
- photo provided by Patsy McComas

199

to – Roy and Dale

I love you both. You were so important in my life and my greatest influence. I'm a 53-year-old wife and mother—gram, too. I've been blessed with a wonderful life, and I'm so glad I had you in it as my role models! I've written to you before. I sent a collage of your pictures to the Portsmouth Museum a few years ago, and in my home I have my own Roy and Dale Museum. It's a large collection that I have, and I just recently purchased a Roy Rogers pony saddle! YES!!!! My first letter was mailed to you when I was about 10 (1953.) I wanted you to come to Maine to do personal appearances, and I even offered you my field! I guess I've always been an optimist with a huge imagination. I love you. You were, and always will be, my heroes.

Betty Horton, Bridgton, ME - 1/15/96

Roy Rogers Arcade Card
- provided by Miriam Hoeffler

to - Roy

I am 72 years old. I forgot the year I received the photo. I left Harrisburg, Pennsylvania in 1949, and I got the photo while I was in Harrisburg. It was a long time ago. Tell Dale Evans, your wife, that I listen to her on the radio, and I enjoy her show. God bless you, Roy. God bless you.

Miriam Hoeffler, Vega Alta, Puerto Rico - 10/11/96

All Hat and No Cattle – My Love Affair With The West

When Roy Rogers and Trigger galloped into my life, our home in rural Connecticut backed up to woods, the ideal yard for kids still using their imaginations. No video games for us! That small version of the Silver Screen fed our imaginations and provided all the sparks we needed to create our own stories. My dream Palomino and me were riding with Roy Rogers and Dale Evans, protecting the innocent and roundin' up the bad guys. Didn't we look grand in our hats and twin holsters? Sons of the Pioneers records played on our new Motorola stereo. *Gunsmoke, Bonanza*, and my Mom's favorite, *Have Gun Will Travel* filled our nighttime TV screen. All aired past my bedtime and I lay awake listening to the thrilling theme music, feverishly imaging what was happening! A friend of the family gave me my first nickname, "Slim Jim," and I spent hours dreaming of riding the wide open range.

Little did I know how these early embers of "first loves" would be rekindled. If anyone had told me, during the first thirty years of my life, that a career in the midst of both the "real" and "reel" West awaited me, I would have denied it. Enthusiastically embracing the corporate retail world and moving fast up the ladder, I thought I had it made. But, like all page-turning stories, mine was full of twisted paths, unexpected opportunities and cliffhangers. Jump forward to the early 1990s. California beckoned, and like so many before us, my husband Jim and I moved west. Scared to trade the familiar East Coast for the unknown West, I began to read women's diaries that chronicled their 19th Century overland travel experience. I soon discovered I had no reason to complain, as my journey would be so much easier.

In February of 1991 I rendezvoused with my childhood love...the landscape of the imaginary West and the heroes that rode across it. One visit to the Gene Autry Museum of Western Heritage, now known as the Autry National Center, and I fell passionately in love. Within a week I was volunteering and within a year sharing its collections with students and visitors from around the world. The West was under my skin, changing me from the inside out. Old habits and interests were replaced with all things Western. Luckily, my husband was equally enthralled. We read Western history, listened to Western music, and chose Western style for home and wardrobe. Within a few years I was invited to join the staff and share Gene's dream of presenting both the historical and mythical stories of the West to the world. I was in heaven!

Fast forward to 2011. Now settled into OutWest Western Boutique and Cultural Center, our very own piece of the West, we continue our dream of exploring and presenting the West. Following the lead of those who came before us, the dreamers and doers, we are privileged to share our journey with historians, authors, artists, musicians, designers, craftsmen, and performers of all types. We consider ourselves, "all hat and no cattle," yet our dedication to preserving and showcasing the West is true. We set up shop in 2007 on the new frontier, the Internet. Missing the opportunity to share the West's stories in a personal way, we opened our first store front in 2009. OutWest's home is on the Walk of Western Stars in Old Town Newhall in California. Begun in 1981, these bronze and terrazzo tiles honor the legends of Western film, television and radio who have contributed to America's heritage since 1900. Our block begins with the tiles honoring Gene Autry, Tom Mix, and William S. Hart. Roy Rogers and Dale Evans are just up the block. OutWest sits between Rex Allen and Riders In The Sky – the perfect place to be as we are the bridge between the old and new West. William S. Hart's historic home is at the end of our block. The annual Santa Clarita Cowboy Festival, attended by thousands, is held each April on the grounds of Gene Autry's film studio, Melody Ranch. OutWest is heaven to us!

Take a lesson from Tom Mix and Tony, Gene Autry and Champion, Roy Rogers and Trigger – saddle up and ride! There's nothing as exciting and life changing as a life in The West.

Bobbi Jean Bell, OutWest Western Boutique and Cultural Center on the Walk of Western Stars, Newhall, CA, Home of "SCVTV Presents The OutWest Concert Series"

Jim Bell, Bobbi Jean Bell surrounded by The Tumbling Tumbleweeds
Tumbleweeds left to right: Babyface R.J. Mills, Smokin' Dan Dungan, Tumbleweed Rob
Wolfskill, Big Cade Parenti and Chris Acuff
- photo provided by Bobbi Jean Bell and The Tumbling Tumbleweeds

A Slye Light Guides the Way

I originally wrote this piece for the Western Music Association's celebration of Roy's 100th birthday and am honored to now be able to share my thoughts with all Roy's fans.

When all is said and done it's the pictures and sounds lingering in our minds that help compose who we will become, and if we pay close attention to where these sounds and pictures are pointing we can eventually discover the path to making our dreams come true. Some of these early signposts for me were the influences of Roy Rogers—not directly to me, but to the influence he had on my parents and grandparents.

Growing up in the metropolis of Los Angeles, California was no easy feat. There are in fact many dangers and many negative influences that can easily consume those with insufficient light to guide them through what is known as "the concrete jungle." Through this turbulent and sometimes volatile maze of hustle and bustle there were always glimpses of something magical and transportive, hinting to me that there was yet another path that may be taken. The sound of cowboys singing in harmony from the television on a Saturday morning, or my Grandmother bursting out in an astonishingly "spot on" yodel – that these conspicuously striking sounds emanated from any place in urban Los Angeles carved an image somewhere deep in my soul that there is someplace beautiful and unique waiting for me to explore someday.

Later, as a young man, it became clear to me that singing and music was my passion and it was then that these early markers became the framework of a dream I have followed. It was that glinty-eyed cowboy who sang and yodeled in the hearts of my grandmother and my parents who had been pointing the way even before I came into the world. Now as an adult I can simply refer to this great American hero known as Roy Rogers as a model of not only excellent musicianship but as the standard for what is the best in men. It was his appeal all along that remained a distant yet steady light, gently guiding me through the fog of uncertain youth that, once lifted, revealed a beacon that shone on my very own destiny.

Thank you, Roy, for not only delighting my parents but for also, through them, showing me the way to who I was to become. You are my hero!

Tumbleweed Rob Wolfskill
The Tumbling Tumbleweeds: Western Music Association Crescendo Award Winners and Academy of Western Artists Duo/Group of the Year

Blaze Across the West CD
- provided by Tumbling Tumbleweeds

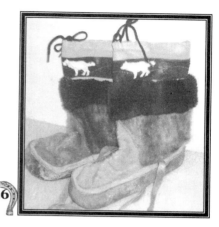

45 **46**

to – Roy and Dale

You were the best in everything you ever did. I named my oldest daughter, Dale Ann, born in 1955, after Dale, and my youngest son, Roy, born in 1966, after you, Roy. In fact, when he was a youngster and I told my doctor about how my son got his name, he would always write out his prescriptions for "Roy Rogers." Since I lived in a small town, the druggist got a big kick out of it. My little Roy is now 29 years old and a banquet manager who loves helping people celebrate. My father is 81 years old, and I will be bringing him to California to visit with his sisters. We plan to go to your museum. Please get well and meet us there! I think of you both so often, and I'm also looking forward to meeting your son and other family, too. Do you know how many people love you all? Too many to count!

Elizabeth Ann Evon, Bridgewater, NJ - 10/9/96

to – Roy

You were my first love. As I wished on a star every morning and every night it was to meet you one day. In 1978-79 I was living in Pennsylvania, and while driving through Monroeville, PA I noticed a sign that said you were opening a restaurant on there. I stood in line for hours to shake your hand. Miracles do come true! If I don't meet you here on earth again, I know I'll see you and Dale in Heaven, which I believe won't be too far in the future.

Caroll Byrd, Lenoir City, TN - 11/8/90

to – Roy

I know you don't remember me, but when I was about 6, I met you at Santa Anita Race Track. What a thrill! I believe my family saw every movie you ever made. My dad, a great western lover, was Graceton Philpot, and he trained thoroughbreds for L.B. Mayor, Lou Costello, and others. You may remember him or my grandparents, W.B. (Bill) and Margaret Finnegan. Grandpa also trained horses. What great times the early 40s were. Cowboy idol, Allan (Rocky) Lane, spent a lot of time in our home in Arcadia and told me you drank brandy in your milk out in public so the boys and girls would know milk was good for them. Whether it was true or not remains to be seen. Allan was probably just trying to make points since he asked me to marry him, too. At age 6, he really made an impression, and I couldn't wait to grow up. However time goes by quickly, and I married in 1955, have 2 boys who are married, and 4 beautiful granddaughters. So in 35 years I've lost track of Allan. Alas, he probably forgot me anyway. Roy, growing up with you makes you a part of the family. You and Dale have been such an inspiration to so many. It's strange writing to someone you've met only a couple of times but feel like you've known a lifetime. Two years ago our little town got cable TV. One of the old westerns starred both you and Allan Lane. I got so interested I was late getting to our store! But what memories. I wish you well and many Happy Trails.

Lewellyn Frey, Stapleton, NE - 11/21/90

to – Roy and Dale

You have been such an inspiration and role model for children. Our kids grew up watching your movies, and Roy, your famous "May the Good Lord take a likin' to you" has been my husband's favorite expression throughout life, and he uses it a lot. We ask that the Lord keep you both in his care and someday, somewhere, we'll meet and we'll all sing together!

Bill and Louise Proffitt, Van Wert, OH - 10/12/96

206

to – Dale

I have thought of you many times over the last few months, and I wish that there was a better way for me to express the respect and affection that I have always felt for you and for Roy. I will always be thankful to Dusty for making sure that I had the opportunity to spend some time with Roy when I lived in Apple Valley. I told Roy once that it was a real treat just to be able to shake his hand and see the twinkle in his eyes when he smiled. He was always very kind to me, and I will treasure the memories of his friendship for the rest of my life. I think it is important for those of us who grew up with you and Roy as role models to expose our younger generations to your work so that they might also accept the values you represent. I don't think I can offer any wisdom that might make this time easier for you, but I just want you to know that you and your family are in my thoughts and prayers, and I hope this note has found you well and that each of your days brings you peace and contentment. I am always your fan and always your friend.

Don Morecraft, Linton, IN - 10/14/98

to – Roy

I am a baby boomer, born in 1945, and one of my first wonderful memories is of you and Dale singing "Happy Trails to You." You will always be in millions of people's hearts because you and Dale represent "pure goodness," something very few people of today know about. You've both lived such a wonderful life, setting example after example of what God meant us to be like. I still watch your reruns, and when I do my heart just fills with happiness. Life seemed so simple. You both made it seem like real life was all about loving and raising a wonderful family, having faith and believing it could be an adventure. You were right, and you are proof of it. I love you even though I've never met you. You give me peace and harmony.

Kris Cummings, Weston, FL - 10/1/96

to – Roy

As a child growing up in the sixties you always served as a hero to me, and I still have fond memories of when I would color you and Trigger in my Roy Rogers coloring book. I still have a set of Roy Rogers six guns, a harmonica and cowboy annual book. My family and I still enjoy watching you on television as we have several movies of yours as well as seeing the Roy Roger Theater every Saturday afternoon. You always stood for justice in your shows in a clean and respectable manner in which I still encourage my children to observe, as today we have very few wholesome figures such as yourself to look up to. I always wanted to be like you when I grew up, and now I have a chance to thank you for being a still-very-memorable part of my life. I am one of your biggest fans. Thanks for all the good memories!"

Tim Gallagher and Family, Espanola, Ontario, Canada - 11/22/90

Roy and Trigger fording the Red River

"Roy and Trigger fording the Red River" publicity photo
- photo provided by Tim Gallagher

to – Roy

Happy Birthday, Roy Rogers! May this special day bring you much joy and happiness.
Peter Sands, Hayward, CA - 11/5/90

11/90.
Sandsmark

Roy Rogers hand-drawn birthday card by Peter Sands
- provided by Peter Sands

---

to – Dale

Roy's passing felt like the loss of a lifelong friend. I met him only once in 1955. He was riding Trigger at the time in a rodeo. I shook Roy's hand and pet Trigger. It was a wonderful moment for me, and remains so to this day. He was a wonderful human being and a very positive and good influence on my life. I grew up to become a police officer and retired as Chief of Police. All three of my children are decent, hardworking, moral and caring adults. Of course, I proudly take credit for that, sharing that credit with my wife. However I feel that Roy was a part of this, too, because I believed him, and in him, as my first role model. I, too, own and ride horses and live a country life. I loved Roy and will miss him very much. I wish you comfort and happiness in these thoughts of love. They are most sincere.
Richard Hammler, Newton, NJ - 1/27/99

My love of being a cowboy started in 1938 when a cowboy named Mr. Brown came by the house riding his Palomino. Right then and there I was hooked on being a cowboy. Then soon after Mr. Brown, Gene Autry came into my life.

I first fell in "awe" of Gene Autry when I was about 8 years old. I learned every Gene Autry song by heart and sang my days away. I wanted to be a singing cowboy just like Gene, and over the years I committed even the smallest details of his life to memory. I even remember one time, (much later, in 1960,) when Gene's sidekick, Smiley Burnette, parked his car and forgot to set the brake. Me and Smiley ran after the car as it rolled away, with me shouting, "Smiley the car is rolling away! Let's go after it!" I got to the car first and stopped it. It was pretty funny.

Then there was the day in 1940 when Tom Mix came to Ravenna, OH. He rode into the circus tent on his horse, Tony, Jr., and the thrill of the cowboy life grabbed me even stronger. I and some other kids went to the hotel where Tom was staying, and when Tom came out, he took one look at me, picked me up, and put me on his shoulders. I got to play my harmonica for Tom as he carried me around town. He came to the house and asked my mother if he could take me to Hollywood, but Mother said "no." She thought I was far too young to go off looking for the cowboy life. Sadly, Tom Mix died in a car accident just two weeks after I played my harmonica for him. Then in 1942, when I was about 13 years old, Gene Autry went off to war, and Roy Rogers came to my attention in a big way.

I started liking Roy, so I started looking for pictures and clippings of him. That's when I started my first scrapbook. Roy was very likeable. His voice, his style, his morals and his stature so impressed me. In no time I was active in the Roy Rogers Fan Club, and I guess you could say that Roy Rogers was responsible for part of my life—my family. My wife and I have been married 55 years, but we met more than half a century ago as pen pals in the Roy Rogers fan club. We'd never met in person until 1956. I was drafted into the Army in 1950 and served 7 ½ years, but our correspondence never ceased, and I played my harmonica for her over the telephone. Soon, the words we exchanged turned from mutual admiration for Roy to a love for each other. And once we met in person, we never looked back. Would I have ever met the wonderful woman in my life if not for Roy? I guess we'll never know. But a mutual passion for Roy Rogers turned out to be a pretty strong base on which to build a lifelong relationship. It has certainly worked well for me and my wife and our beautiful children. And amazingly, we still have the love letters we exchanged so long ago.

In 1948, years before I married, was the first time I met Roy. It was at the Roy Rogers Championship Rodeo in Chicago. Roy invited his fan club and had all the fans take a bow. It was such a treat. The second time I met Roy and Dale was in 1950 at the Warwick Hotel in New York City. I brought flowers for Dale, and presented them to her. Roy's publicity manager set up that meeting. Then later, I won Roy's only signature shirt in a fan club contest and I wore it at the Convention Center in Columbus, Ohio, where I met Roy and Dale for the third time in 1954.

It was in 1948 when I became the Ranch Boss for the Roy Rogers Fan Club for the whole state of Ohio, and I even still today I have the rubber stamp I used at the time that reads: **Frank "Poncho" Fiore – Roy Rogers Fan Club – Ranch Boss of Ohio.** That fan club was such an important part of my life and such an important part of the building of my character. To this day, I possess 72 scrapbooks of Roy's life. Once a fan, always a fan.

Although I learned other skills and enjoyed other achievements throughout my life, the cowboy in me has lived on. I was born in 1929, and I'm still living my cowboy dream. To my fans, I'm known as "Francis – God's Cowboy." That's an honor that would never have existed if not for Mr. Brown, Gene, Tom, and Roy Rogers—the man who was, and will always be, the King of the Cowboys to me.

Singing Cowboy, Frank "Frankie Flash" Fiore, Victorville, CA

Frank "Frankie Flash" Fiore with Roy and Dale and that winning Roy Rogers shirt!
- all photos provided by Frank Fiore

to – Roy and Dale

THEN (10/23/96): You are like family to me, and you don't even know me! My husband, John, and I have been married 29 years, and we came from different parts of California, but we have a childhood memory together—Roy and Dale! I guess I better confess a little girl's dream of one day marrying Roy Rogers. But I soon learned as I grew older that there was a lady named Dale in your life. Whenever the neighborhood kids got together to play they knew I was always Dale Evans. The would say, "I know. I know. If Elaine can't be Dale, she isn't going to play." My dad looks a lot like you, Roy. I always told my friends that my dad looks like Roy Rogers. They would all laugh and say, "Yeah, right." One of your movies was playing, and though we didn't have much money, we managed to find enough for a Roy Rogers movie, and Mama would make sandwiches, popcorn and soda pop for the day. The whole week I was counting the days until Saturday night. That night I found my friends, and they wanted to see my daddy. We walked to the car, and my friends couldn't believe how much he looks like you! They wanted to know if he could sing! Daddy wanted to know what I said to my friends, and I told him that I'd said my dad looked just like Roy Rogers. Dad just smiled because he and Mom both knew how special Roy and Dale were to me. I know you both hear this all the time, but here goes again. You've been such a big part of my life. You are both good people, like my parents. I hope to make it to your museum to see my childhood heroes in person. There is a small little cowgirl in this fifty-two year old woman who still cherishes her Roy and Dale. I hope you feel our big hug!

NOW (7/1/11): One Christmas Dad was only working a couple days a week, and Mama said Christmas was going to be small. It was small, but wonderful, too! My gift was a Dale Evans gun and holster set. Boy! Did I think I was something! We are both seniors now, but still remember our childhood with Roy, Dale, Trigger, Buttermilk, Bullet, Gabby, Pat, Nellybelle, and the Sons of the Pioneers. Our retirement has meant we get to go camping, and around the campfire Roy and Dale still find their way into our conversations. Many great stories of them are told around the old campfire even today."
Elaine and John Hoyt, Byron, CA

to – Roy

It's hard to adequately thank someone for so much! I am sure there are many millions of us out here who can no longer look at a western landscape or listen to a western song without thinking of you. You have not only personified, far better than anyone else ever could, all that is best in the great historic American western legend, but you have added your own great talent, wit, charm and integrity, in short, your own personality, to that legend forever. I was horribly bullied as a shy child. When you are just beginning to develop an idea of your place in the world, it is devastating to have howling mobs following you around, screaming that they hate you. Fortunately, I had discovered the Roy Rogers TV show by then, and it was such a comfort to know that there were people in the outside world who cared about others and treated people (even the "bad guys") with respect as they stood up for what was right (against bullies.) Roy, you gave me hope that someday I would find friends and that the world would not always be so hostile. Many, many thanks for the many wonderful things you did for so many people.

a fan, Kendall Park, NJ - 11/17/90

to – Roy

At this Thanksgiving season, I wanted to take this opportunity to thank you for the many hours of pleasure you have given to me over the years, through your shows and your singing, and through being you. As a small child you were always my hero. As I grew older, it meant even more to me to learn that my hero was not only a hero on the screen, but a hero in real life as well. I wish you and your family a wonderful Thanksgiving filled with God's love and blessings.

Patsy Stringer, Arcadia, LA - 11/19/90

to – Roy

   I'm 51 years old and have been a Roy Rogers fan since I was a kid. I was one of those kids who went to the Saturday matinee to see every new Roy Rogers movie. I had a special treat when I was ten years old. My father took me to see your personal appearance show at Hobart Arena in Troy, OH. That's something I've never forgotten. Of course I watched all your shows on TV and continued to be a fan along with my brother who is ten years younger than me. In 1980 my husband, two daughters and myself took a family vacation to California. I requested a stop in Victorville to visit your museum. To my great delight you were there that day filming the P.M. Magazine TV show. I was thrilled to be able to shake hands with my favorite cowboy. My husband took a picture of you with my daughters and me. I'm very proud of that picture and had it made into an 8 x 10, framed it, and hung it on my family room wall. It's been hanging there since 1980 and is quite the conversation piece. Even my daughter's 21-year-old friends are impressed when they see it. Next spring I hope to be able to attend the Roy Rogers Festival in Portsmouth. I've been wanting to do that for several years. In closing, I just want to say thank you for giving me someone to enjoy and admire for the past forty years. I think it's important to have heroes, and I've had one in you all my life. I'm not sure kids of today can or will be able to say that when they grow up. To me you will always be the "King of the Cowboys." God bless you and your family!
Pat Arnold, Springboro, OH - 11/13/90

Pat Arnold and daughters with Roy Rogers
- photo provided by Pat Arnold

215

to – Roy

You don't know me, but I met you when you opened your restaurant in Monroeville, PA. It was one of the greatest joys of my life to shake the hand of Roy Rogers. As a kid I grew up dreaming of being a cowboy, but never in my wildest dreams did I ever think I would ever meet the greatest cowboy of all. I still have your picture that you autographed for me. Even though I may never hear from you, I want you to know that to me, you are truly the "King of the Cowboys." I will never forget the memories. I will cherish them always.
Carol Chilcoat, Pittsburgh, PA – undated

to – Roy

As a girl in Hawaii, I went to see you at the airport, but I was too chicken to shake your hand. You and Mrs. Rogers meant so much to me growing up, as at times my home wasn't happy. But for each and every one of us growing up with you, you made our lives better. I work with a fellow that was in the service. You sang for him, and he kept asking you to play songs he would name. So here is another person you did something for. It really is the little things that make the biggest memories. We love you. I have never written a note to a person in show business before. I hope I said things right. May God bless and keep you, and may you and your family have a wonderful holiday.
Kathy Grace, Vallejo, CA - 11/6/90

Dorothy Kaiser
-photo provided by Dorothy Kaiser

to – Roy

You have brought sunshine into the lives of millions of people, both young and old. May it be returned to you twofold. Family and friends have always remarked how much I looked like Dale. I enjoy hearing it. All the love, help and support that you gave to youth over the years has had a large influence in my own life to help and enjoy working with youth. I plan to continue to do so as long as my health permits. My husband, Denver, and I send you our love and remember you in our prayers.

Dorothy and Denver Kaiser, Barnesville, OH - 10/26/90

to – Roy

My mother took this photo of us together in 1945. The back of our property adjoined the back of yours in North Hollywood. We lived on Ethel Avenue. I just loved to go down and see Trigger and the other horses, and you were always so nice if you were there. You let me ride the Triggers and were always kind. What a little girl's dream I lived. Just a thrill.

Nancy Walsh, Olympia, WA - 11/29/90

1945 - Nancy Walsh with Roy Rogers
- photo provided by Nancy Walsh

217

to – Dale

I once rode in the Houston Rodeo Parade next to you and Roy when I was a kid. That was such a special time. I patterned my life after Roy's because he not only told us how it was, he walked the walk. My dad's name was Roy. My name is Roy. And I had a golden palomino I raised as a boy whose name, naturally, was "Trigger." Had I not been inspired in my youth by Roy Rogers and Dale Evans, I probably would not have followed my dream and been motivated to get into a broadcasting career by age 16 as the youngest radio person in Texas at that time. Nor would I have competed and won to become the voice of the 50-foot cowboy icon known as "Big Tex". When something good happens, I think of you, Roy, and Happy Trails. I hope you enjoy my poem:

The Meaning of Life by Rea Roy "Sonny" Stolz

Life: what purpose have you now,
To live each day for why and how?
Or, embrace in faith a gentle yoke,
With a spirit committed to devote?

Have you a plan, a dream or skill,
Which brings to each and all no ill?
Do you undertake the one path walk,
Or, do you merely talk that talk?

Is there a time, an appointed hour,
When you seek to draw His power?
Can it be said of you by all,
This one truly hears the call?

When wrong is done or errors made,
Do you step forward in the fray?
Have you limits within your game,
Does truth win over carnal reign?

Is the tongue shown you are master,
Or, do you spew banal ever faster?
If some friend in you confided,
Would the trust soon be derided?

Have you stopped and paused today,
To bow and take the time to pray?
Can you forgive, can you forget,
Every trespass, every debt?

Are your things stacked and piled,
To keep your soul un-reconciled?
Is happiness some pale illusion,
The spirit dying for an infusion?

Would you, could you slip away,
To follow Him, waste not a day?
Or, are you mired into a quest,
Chasing some lowly second best?

Did you not listen to the preacher
Or, hear your Mother as your teacher?
And if the One who calls is faithful,
Should you be less than willing able?

Be not confused to what this means,
The world 'tis never what it seems,
Yet, free's the answer from above,
The meaning of life? Simply: Love.

Rea Roy "Sonny" Stolz, Houston, TX - 12/21/98

to – Roy

My admiration for you goes back as far as I can remember, and I am 55 years old. My best friend and I have been friends all our lives, and we are both avid Roy Rogers fans. Our friendship has lasted even though we have lived 155 miles apart ever since we were teenagers. Our respect and admiration for you is just as strong. As young girls we rejoiced with you, mourned with you, and in one of those "school girl crush" periods, said we were going to Hollywood to "be with you." What fantasies! Then we grew up, dated, married and had families. Several years ago my friend and I and our husbands were driving in California and came upon your museum. What a thrill! A couple of years later we went through it again. What great memories! I so enjoy seeing you and Dale on TV even now, though the times that it happens are far too rare. I'm always amazed at how great your singing still sounds and how great you and Dale both still look. I just had to write and thank you for all the pleasure you have given to so many. What would we have done without you?

Frances St. Aoro, St. Paul, MN - 11/8/90

to – Roy and Dale

Roy, you can't be suffering from old age because you are only 84. You are still a young man in my eyes! A few of us were down at the Roy Rogers and Dale Evans Museum last year, and I thought you looked great, as handsome as ever. All of us had our picture made with you. My daughter cried like a baby she was so happy and thrilled to get to see you. You are her favorite, and she just didn't think it would ever happen. We asked where Dale was, and you said you made her stay home to clean house. Is that right, Dale? ha ha! I hope you both know how much you are loved. I know I love you.

Lucy Trevino, Hanford, CA - 9/30/96

to – Dale

I am 48 years old, raised in Houston, Texas. I've "known" Dale Evans and Roy Rogers since I was born! As a child, I never missed a Saturday with you. I loved those Houston Stock Shows and Rodeos when you performed at the old Houston Coliseum. Of course, as a kid, I always carried a Roy Rogers lunch kit to school. You are truly part of my roots. I can tell that you are humbled by the knowledge that God has blessed you with a special talent and huge audience to share your faith and your blessings with—what a tremendous honor and responsibility, which you have faithfully, beautifully assumed. I am a "career" Little League baseball coach. That is my ministry. Occasionally when talking to the kids about the "old days" I'll ask if they know who Roy Rogers is. I'm saddened to tell you that virtually all 6 to 15-year-olds have no idea. It's a sad commentary on America that Dale Evans and Roy Rogers is not still on TV every Saturday morning. What a tremendous heritage you provided If only it could continue. At one of our Little League tournaments we had the help of some Navy R.O.T.C. boys (high school age.) They were earning public service credits. For fun, I told three of the cadets, "I'll give $20 to the first one who can sing "Anchors Away." None of them had even heard of it! So, as a consolation prize, I said, "Okay, I'll give the same $20 to the first one who can tell me who Roy Rogers is." Well, they thought and they thought. Finally one of them spoke up, *"That's that place where you get that barbeque, isn't it?"* He was referring, I guess, to Roy Rogers Roast Beef. I laughed until I couldn't breathe! But it was truly sad in my eyes, and I'm saddened that my own kids (20, 16 and 13) have grown up without knowing the influence of Roy Rogers and Dale Evans. Dale, you and Roy are gifts that millions were lucky enough to receive.
David Reese, Richmond, TX - 1/11/99

to – Roy

Oodleaydeoo – no – *yodel-lay-de-oooooo*!!
Is this how it's done? I can just hear you!
Harriet – (no address)

to – Roy and Dale

THEN (9/30/96): Both of you have been "stars" to me since I was young. I am from a farming community in Southwestern Oklahoma and have lived in this part of the world all my life. Entertainment for me as a young teenager was basically what went on at church and at the movies at a small town theater, "The Rex," in Sentinel, Oklahoma. Oh how my brothers and sisters would work just to get to go on Saturday afternoon to the show. How we thrilled at the clean Roy and Dale movies we saw, the bad guys brought to justice and Dale finally choosing Roy to ride off with into the future singing "Happy Trails to You!" Roy and Dale, I remember December 31, 1947 probably as well as you do. You see, it is also my wedding anniversary. Allen and I had chosen that date before we knew you were planning a wedding that day. Wasn't the weather horrible? But it could have been worse. Our wedding was in a small country church three miles from Rocky, Oklahoma, not so very far from your own Oklahoma wedding. We are also still together and have proudly told others it was a good day because Roy and Dale have had a lasting marriage also! We are admiring fans who have loved you "through the years."

NOW (6/30/11): We have now been married nearly 64 years. When we married we were young and in love. Now I am 81 and Allen is 89 years young, and though we have never been wealthy, God has been good to us and we feel the wealth that He blessed us with!

Lola and Allen Diffendaffer, Rocky, OK

Allen and Lola Diffendaffer
- photo provided by Lola Diffendaffer

51 Roy and Dale Wedding Spoon
Married December 31, 1947

to – Roy

I've always been a very ardent fan of yours. I wrote you and Dale back in the 60s and you were so nice to answer my note and thank me for finding my kind of letter in your ranch mailbox. You also sent a signed photo of both you and Dale. I have that photo still. You have done so much for so many and shown love to so many. I for one thank you for the many years that you've given me the strength to do things. May God bless you and Dale always.
Shirley Leavitt, Oak Ridge, NJ - 11/8/90

Dear Friend:
Thank you for writing. We hope you like this picture of the whole "gang" as much as we enjoy finding mail like yours in the ranch mail box.
Many Happy Trails,
Roy, Dale, Pat & Bullet

1963 – Shirley Leavitt

Shirley Leavitt photo,
Riders Club photo, and autographed
Roy and Dale photo,
provided by Shirley Leavitt

to – Roy

I am writing this for my brother, Johnny. He is challenged and can't write except for his name. He is 58 years old but his mind is like a young boy. He is so sweet and loving, and ever since he heard you had been sick in the hospital, he has been so worried. He asks me every day if I've heard anything about you. He wants you to feel better. You have not made a movie that he hasn't seen, and he watches your reruns on TV over and over. He just loves Roy, Dale and Gabby. So Johnny is sending all his love and prayers from his house to yours. He wants to take care of you.

Johnny Towns, (with help from his sister who loves him) Bartlesville, OK - 11/9/90

to – Roy

You were my hero when I was growing up. I lived, ate, and slept Roy Rogers and Dale Evans. I had more cowboy hats and broom horses than you could shake a stick at. And my Roy Rogers and Dale Evans lunchbox was the most! I think "Happy Trails" was the only song I could really sing. I remember one time a neighbor's horse got loose, and it came into our yard. I was delighted. I was finally going to have my "Trigger." But Mom made me give it back! Oh, how I wanted that horse. You and Dale have done wonders for the world with your kindness and gentleness. I know you have had more than your share of tragedies in your lives, and I always admired how you both went on and reached out to help other people through your own pain. You never felt sorry for yourselves. And I think the most impressive of all is how the Hollywood life never seemed to influence you. You were both always so kind and such great role models. I can still close my eyes and see the black and white TV with the two of you singing as you sat on your horses. I wish my boys had heroes from TV such as you. I'll never forget that special smile, your bright and warm eyes, and of course, your COWBOY HAT!

Christine Toops, Lake Oswego, OR - 11/19/90

to – Roy

I always refer to you as Roy when I refer to you with friends and relations, but never having been introduced, I believe that it is correct to refer to you by your proper name, So, Mr. Rogers, let me start by saying my name is Lou, and you have always been my hero. I'm about 45, give or take a week, and when I was young, "45" was a caliber of a six-shooter. Back then we were all good guys, and you were the chief good guy, someone that all us little good guys could rally behind with pride. Well, we're a tad older now, but not so old that we don't need heroes anymore. And, Mr. Rogers, you still fit that bill. Heroes are hard to come by, and I don't count many in my life. I'm still trying to be that clean living man that you long ago inspired. You're still my hero, and I need you. You have been an inspiration for me to always do the right thing. I haven't always been able to do that, but I sure try to. Having a model like you makes it easier to pick a more straight and narrow path, and I hope that your good influence will be felt and copied by upcoming role models for the generations after me. I know that I can't always live up to your standards, but in my own small way, I try to set the type of example that you might be proud of. But since I know that I really can't always get it right, I'd like to extend an invitation to come to Brooklyn, NY and give this younger generation a first hand look at what a real gentleman and a proper example of a man looks like. Hey, maybe some of it will rub off on them, the way some of it rubbed off on me! This letter comes with love and best wishes, for the world needs life examples like those set by you and your lovely wife, Dale. God love and keep you.

Louis Ferrier, Brooklyn, NY - 11/2/96

52

224

to – Roy

You and Dale have always been special to me. I met you briefly, or shall I say shook your hand, when you were in Springfield, Massachusetts in 1958. I didn't get to speak to you. And on two occasions as I faced death, my wish and my prayer was, "Oh, Lord, I wish I could have met them and talked to them." But our lives and paths would never cross. Through the years I've lifted you folks to the throne of God many, many times. May God continue to bless you both, and although I may never see you here, one day in Glory we shall meet.

Mary Jacobs, Winchester, NH - 10/23/90

to – Dale

Last year we were at the museum and got to meet and talk with Roy. This was a wonderful experience for us. We were on an 8-week trip form North Carolina to California, and talking with Roy was the highlight of our trip. You were in the hospital at the time and I asked Roy if he would give you an angel that I had made. He said he would and that he knew you would like it. We just wanted you to know how much it meant to us to meet such a fine person.

Ruth and Ertle King, Huntersville, NC - 9/39/98

to – Roy and Dale

You have always been my heroes—great people and great parents. I've raised six children myself, one of my own. I am a single mother and have my precious 86-year-old mother living with me. I'm happy that I have people around me who care about me just as I care very much about them. When I was 16, my parents and I were driving from Hannibal, MO, and I saw a white truck and horse trailer. Dad honked and you guys waved! It made my day and my life! I am very close to God, and I have always prayed for you and your family. You bless this world. There are no heroes like you today.

Juanita Coe, Marceline, MO - 10/2/96

to – Dale

In April, 1945, it was my good fortune to spend an entire day with Roy Rogers here in Pittsburgh while he was on a personal appearance tour. I was 17 years old at the time and an ardent racing pigeon fancier, as he was. He took all of that day off so that we could spend time together talking about our pigeons and visiting several local lots and pigeon clubs. In the evening he took me to the rodeo where he was appearing. Being able to spend this much time with Roy Rogers was a teenager's dream come true. I am 71 years old now and have never forgotten that very special day 53 years ago. About 11 years ago I managed a few moments with Roy once again while he was in Pittsburgh as the Grand Marshal of the University of Pittsburgh's 200-Year Anniversary celebration. You have lost a great guy, Dale, a modest, unassuming, sincere man. The millions who have followed Roy and Dale these many years will forever remember the good that he has contributed to this world, as well as those, like myself, who were privileged to touch Roy's life in a very small way.
Bernard Lefkowitz, Pittsburgh, PA - 9/10/98

to – Roy

I've been a fan for a long time. Remember the friendly old rivalry between you and Gene Autry? We fans would divide into two groups depending which of you we thought was the best. I was always in the Rogers Club. I'm soon going to be 62 and I'm still a faithful fan, but now I've added Dale, too. I've always been a fan of hers, too. I'm so happy you are together. I liked you being a team, and I enjoyed your movies together. I miss the original Sons of the Pioneers. I'm sure I can hear faint sounds from up yonder when they sing. Sometimes I stand outside looking up at the star-studded sky and I think I can hear the sound of old cowboy tunes. Maybe it's my imagination working overtime. I'm a dreamer of the good old days. Some of them really were the best. May the good Lord keep you around for a long time so you can enjoy life, and we can enjoy you. And may you and Dale be together always.
Betty Lorah, Fostoria, OH - 12/20/90

to – Dale

I was just writing to wish you a happy 86th birthday. Next year me and my family are supposed to take a trip to the Grand Canyon and then on to the Roy Rogers and Dale Evans Museum. I sure hope we get to see you when we do come. I've got three younger sisters, and the youngest one, Amanda, who will be two on November 28, is already saying, "I want to watch Roy Rogers!" Mama says that I brainwashed her, and I guess she's right. I really appreciate all the things that you have done for people everywhere throughout the years. Remember that you are always in my prayers.

Stephanie Landry, Kenbridge, VA - 10/31/98

to – Roy and Dale

Many years ago I attended a rodeo at the armory. It was a wonderful performance, and what made it nicer was how at the closing, both of you rode around the arena with your hand outstretched, touching hands that could be reached. It was such a wonderful thing to do. After a long performance you took the time to thank everyone. Also, Roy announced that the souvenirs that were being sold that day did not benefit the two of you in any way. Since these items were so expensive, I was glad the money was going somewhere needed. I've always wanted to say this, but I didn't know where to mail a letter. We don't seem to have many wholesome performances anymore, and I thank you for your clean, decent shows. Nice people like you make this world a better place. My prayers are with you.

Mary Baird, Louisville, K - 10/10/96

to – Roy

I wanted to write you this letter to let you know just how much I've loved and admired you since I was a little girl. I'm a 44-year-old housewife, and my childhood was based on being able to watch TV every Saturday morning and see all the best shows, of which yours was Number One! How much I would have given to be there with you and Dale on all your adventures. Those were the best days of my life, and I sure wish the kids of today had people like you and Dale to look up to like I did. I felt that since all of you worked for the good and right in life that I should be like that, too. I've grown up trying to treat people fairly and kindly. All of the violence on TV and at the movies today is no good. My sons, ages 21 and 16, do not realize what good shows they have missed by not growing up with my generation. Everything seemed so much better back when I was a girl. People were better. And I know in my heart it was the good guys like you who helped shape and build that goodness in all of us. I guess everyone at some time or another wishes they could go back in time. And I sure do, too. I miss the good old days, and maybe you do, too. I'm lucky to still have my parents. They live upstairs from me and my family, and I take care of them as best I can. My mom is 84 and my dad is 87. My mother tells me all the time about how awful people on TV are today—nothing good to watch. And basically, she's right. There are a few good shows, but if I could change them all for the westerns I loved so much, I would do it in a minute! You may not think anybody even remembers you, but you're in a lot of people's thoughts every single day. We all love you so much and wish the very best for you. I hope I haven't bored you too much but I just had to write down how much I care. God bless you and Dale and keep you well. I will continue to pray for you. I sure do love you a lot.

Glenda Hopkins, St. Louis, MO - 11/9/90

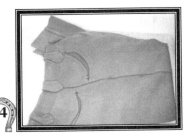

54

to – Roy

Thank you for being an inspiration to so many millions over the years. Our children sent you "feel better" art to make you smile. We hope you do.
John, Terri, Luke, Sunni and Farnum Smart, Wallawalla, WA - 11/20/90

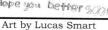

Art by Lucas Smart

Art by Sunni Smart

Art by Farmer Smart

- all art provided by the Smart Family

to – Roy and Dale

Our daughter, Marva, was Maid of Honor at your grandson's wedding (Joyce and Dan Swift.) Dan and I have talked lots about his grandfather. I especially enjoyed the story of Mr. Rogers' disguise just to go to a swap meet, and I loved hearing about his walks. I walk 3 miles a day. My husband and I were both born in Nebraska (came to California in 1956) and have followed your life and your careers. My husband is a marathon runner and wouldn't you know he went to an out-of-town race on Joyce and Dan's wedding day. I know you both attended, and I wish I could have met you both. You are indeed a highly respected couple. God bless and keep you both well. Oh, and Dan says I make potato salad just like his mom!
Monta Powers, Lancaster, CA -10/31/90

to – Dale

As Americans we live in a society where events come and go, and most are soon forgotten. When Roy left this earth my heart was greatly saddened, and for days I experienced a feeling of emptiness. Being a happy person, I knew this feeling would pass, but it hasn't. I never met Roy, but he was my friend. He taught me values and morals that have remained with me in my adult life. He was everything I always wanted to be. Children today are missing a lesson in life by not growing up with mentors like Roy. But it is up to us adults to pass on the legacy that Roy left us—morals, honesty, truth and deep spiritual commitment. Yes, I do miss him, but I know he is better off today than we are. Someday I plan to walk up to him and say, "Howdy, Roy, I always wanted to meet you." I think he'll smile that big smile, and we'll have a long conversation. You know I thought a long time before writing this letter and was sure I would fill it with cowboy quotes and references to the movies. I guess that was a front, and once I started to write, the words just came deep from within my heart. I'm sure glad they did. God bless you, and God bless the King of the Cowboys.
Ted Grooms, West Union, OH - 10/28/98

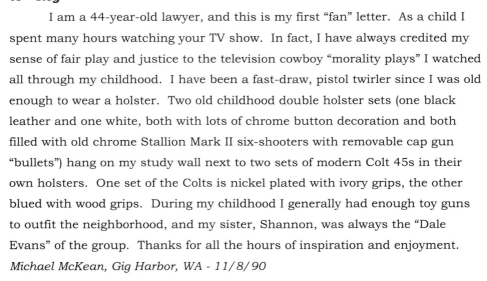

to – Roy

I am a 44-year-old lawyer, and this is my first "fan" letter. As a child I spent many hours watching your TV show. In fact, I have always credited my sense of fair play and justice to the television cowboy "morality plays" I watched all through my childhood. I have been a fast-draw, pistol twirler since I was old enough to wear a holster. Two old childhood double holster sets (one black leather and one white, both with lots of chrome button decoration and both filled with old chrome Stallion Mark II six-shooters with removable cap gun "bullets") hang on my study wall next to two sets of modern Colt 45s in their own holsters. One set of the Colts is nickel plated with ivory grips, the other blued with wood grips. During my childhood I generally had enough toy guns to outfit the neighborhood, and my sister, Shannon, was always the "Dale Evans" of the group. Thanks for all the hours of inspiration and enjoyment.
Michael McKean, Gig Harbor, WA - 11/8/90

to – Roy

My father passed away when I was 10 years old. My mother had to raise me and my 3 brothers. We learned to work hard and help our mother out any way we could. I did a lot of babysitting and other things, like house cleaning and ironing, after I got out of school. I went to all your movies. I wrote down the names of them because I could only afford to go to them one time. I would buy magazines and get the pictures and put them up on my wall in my bedroom. My mother would come in my room and she would say, "I see you have some new pictures up." I told her many times when I would come home from seeing your movies that you and Dale would get married someday. You know what? I was 15 years old when you and Dale got married, and I was so happy for both of you! This is where you both became so important in my life. I looked up to you, Roy, because I had no father, and I knew the things I read about you was right. I knew that you were living a good life, setting a good example for others, and I missed my father very much. I told myself many times that I wanted to be like you and Dale and have a good life. If I could have two sets of parents, I would choose you and Dale. I wished many times that they would have a contest saying to write in why you would like to meet Roy Rogers. I would have written in so fast to see if I could win! I have watched interviews with you on TV, and every time I would tell myself that I should write to you and let you know what I feel, and then I would tell myself that doing so doesn't matter. But I want you to know how much I love you and Dale and how much you helped me throughout my life. I wished so many times I could have been in your family, that you could have been more parents to guide me. I have a wonderful mother. I love her with all my heart, and I know if my dad had lived he would have given me love, too. I want you both to live forever. When I was still in my teens I would tell myself that my mother would live forever because God took my father. I thought that my mother would never grow old. My mother is still alive. She is 88 years old, but as we grow older we learn that no one lives forever. I have a picture of you and Dale. On it you wrote, ""Wilma, Many Happy Trails, Roy Rogers." I received that picture on a day when I was ill with a very bad headache and was down in bed with it. I opened the envelope, and I was so happy! You were my teenage idol, and you're still my idol. I still look up to you both and I love you both with all my heart. I am grateful that you have set a good example for all to see. Someone asked me what I would do if I saw you in person, and I told them that I would give you a "daughter" hug, hold you tight and cry a lot from the happiness of seeing you. I had an uncle who lived in California, and when he came to Utah one time I asked him about you. He told me that if I saw you on the street I would know who you were because there's no one else like you. I am so grateful that you have helped me in my life. I bet it's far more than you know. My love for you is the same today as yesterday. Tears of love, joy and happiness bubble up when I think back to "those days." I will remember you always.

Wilma Packer, Ogden, UT - 11/12/90

to – Roy

I would go to your movies every chance I got. I wanted a horse and guitar just like you and Dale. We lived in a little town of about 200 and our yard was a good acre, plenty of room for a horse I thought (my mother didn't.) I did get a wooden horse I named Trigger and a toy guitar for Christmas, but it wasn't what I had in mind. When I was about 6, and my sister was about 3, we got 2 banty roosters. I named mine Roy Rogers, and my sister's rooster was Gene Autry. When Roy and Gene grew up they got spurs and would fight pretty bad. One day my sister came in with a bloody face. It seems Gene Autry attacked her. The next day they were gone. My dad said a man from a circus came by and said they were so pretty that he wanted them in his circus. My dad gave us each 50 cents from the circus man (big money in those days.) I kept asking for a few years to go find the circus and get Roy back. As for the guitar, I didn't get that either. My mother taught me trombone at age 9. But after graduation I moved to Cedar Rapids and met my husband who played guitar and had a country western band. And you know what? Now I'm a grandmother who sings and plays guitar in a country band...and even the trombone on a few songs!

Sandy Stuefen, Cedar Rapids, IA - 10/2/96

to – Dale

On your first Christmas without Roy, I hope you will be comforted by the memories of your many wonderful years together and the legacy the two of you have provided to generations, here and abroad. We remembered Roy in our Christmas letter this year, and I enclose a copy, sent with all our love.
Wendell and Elaine Johnson, Northbrook, IL - 12/18/98

Roy Rogers remembrance in Johnson's 1998 Christmas Newsletter
- provided by Elaine Johnson

to – Roy and Dale

Writing this letter to you both gives me so much great pleasure. I guess you could say I am one of your "old timers" of long ago in the great past of the 40s and 50s. So many times in my life I have wished I could have seen you in person, but, like you, I grew up poor, but happy in mind and body. Now that I'm way up in age, too, I look back and wish that I could turn back the hands of time. I had little money because my dad was a hard-working man all alone struggling to keep us together, but through it all there was always that happy Saturday afternoon that Daddy always made sure that my sister, brother and me had 12 cents for the movies, 5 cents for a candy bar and 10 cents for popcorn. Those really were the "good old days." You know, Roy, there are millions of us fans who never got to see your museum or to shake your hand or give your lovely wife, Dale, a big hug for all that you have done for us. And one of the greatest gifts you gave was your clean movies with nary a cuss word. You and Dale showed us what's right and good. I wish there was a sweepstakes drawing for all us old timers to win a chance to meet you and Dale. There are still many of us who struggle along, just plain old housewives who have given birth to our wonderful children, teaching them the values that you taught us, like trust and worship. What a wonderful gift it would be to get the chance to meet you! There have been many a happy trail that I have been on in my lifetime, and still, to this day, when I leave a social place, like the Moose Lodge after seeing some friends, I always say "Happy Trails to you, and may the Good Lord take a liking to you." Keep up the wonderful gifts of love, and someday there'll be a big roundup, and we'll see you there. You put so much joy in my heart, and many others, too, and you will forever ride on in our imaginations. Love, hugs and kisses and may God bless you and your family.

Anna Lee and Leroy Gross, Hillsborough, NC - 9/30/96

---

to – Roy

"You are a great guy and a wonderful person. What else is there to say?"

Ada Woodhouse, Malton, Ontario, Canada - 11/5/90

to – Roy

You've always been my favorite cowboy! I'm 43 years old, and every day that you and Dale were on TV, I watched. The only sad time was when you sang Happy Trails. I cried because I thought you weren't coming back. My parents had to try and get my mind on something else a few minutes before your show went off. But it always happened—the tears came. I always loved Trigger. We've had several Palomino horses, and guess their names! I saw you and Trigger in Houston, and I wanted so much to be down in the front row so I could see you better and so that you could grab my hand and say "hi." Now, I've recorded your special early TV years so I will always have you around. I send you my love and wish that you and your children know the kind of love I have with my own dad who is the light of my life. My husband is a favorite man in my life, but fathers and daughters share something special. I wanted to write you this letter and say hang in there for your very special people.
Julie Evoritt Gannon, Eagle Lake, TX - 9/30/96

to – Roy

As a young boy in the 1950s, growing up on a farm and attending a country school, I was able to wear my "guns and holsters" to school so we could play cowboys. The only dispute that ever occurred was who was going to be Roy Rogers. Now with the advent of VHS tapes I am able to buy and rent your movies and television shows and revive those wonderful days of my boyhood. It is truly marvelous to be able to sit down some evenings in front of the television and watch you Roy, with Dale and Pat and Trigger and Bullet and Nellybelle. You are, and always will be, the King of the Cowboys. I am truly a devoted fan.
Jim Ogletree, Brandon, Manitoba, Canada - 11/12/90

to – Roy and Dale

Christmas is upon us once again. It seems that time passes so quickly. Watching "Trail of Robin Hood" has become a Christmas tradition with us. The "Christmas Tree for Johnny" number is my favorite. I take it as being sung for me since I'm a Johnny, too! It is just such a pleasure to watch my heroes in action at the burning bridge. The fight scene must have been interesting to make. We are looking forward to returning to Portsmouth again this year for the Roy Rogers Festival. We have enjoyed it so much these past few years, especially when you returned for your family gathering. This year I'm extra excited because I have lost over 140 pounds and will be able to relax as an average festival cowboy. We hope your schedule will permit your return. And Dale, keep up the excellent shows on TBN. I especially enjoy the shows with family members of movie cowboys, the Sons of the Pioneers, etc. Roy and Dale, you are both wished so much happiness.

Johnny, Sarah and Becky Knight, Orland, IN - undated

to – Dale

I am one of those children who still love you. You made an impact on my life at only 5 years of age, and I will be 50 this June! I have also introduced you both to my children, Joel, 23 and Faith, 20, who have appreciated you also. We were at Anaheim Stadium in 1984 for the Billy Graham Crusade, and my children got the treat of hearing you sing "Happy Trails." Just the mention of that song brings tears to my eyes. I remember when you sang that night at the crusade, the applause just didn't stop! You are both so very loved. How hard it was to lose Roy. Dale, do you know how much you still encourage us? Just to hear you talk about God's peace and His presence in your life helps me so much. I saw you speak in person about 1971 or so, and it was so wonderful. Thank you for all the love you and Roy have poured out of you all of these years. I love you both so much.

Green Bascom, LaHabra, CA – 1/12/99

to – Roy

For quite some time now, I've had it in mind to write to you and tell you how very much I enjoyed your company on Saturday mornings when I was a kid, and I decided it was about time I let you know how much you and Dale meant to me. I was an only child for many years (we adopted my sister when I was 13,) but for the greater potion of those years, we lived on a farm here in Minnesota where I played by myself a lot. I had an old flea-bitten, bay cowpony named Penny who was blind in one eye with a brand on her shoulder and one on her hip, but we "rode the range" together. You and Dale filled our pretend play with many an adventuresome moment. I wish I could express how much I learned from you—good guys and bad guys, right and wrong—those early lessons stuck. Thank you. As the song goes, my heroes will always be cowboys, and you're at the top of my list.

LeeAnn Tietje Christian, Janesville, MN - 10/24/90

1958 – LeeAnn riding Penny
- photo provided by LeeAnn Tietje Christian

to – Roy

Many years ago when I was in grade and high school I went to see your movies, bought your records and spent my allotment from my parents at the Chicago Amusement Park on picture postcards of you, which cost a penny apiece then. My Uncle Oskar was the illustrator for Andy Panda comic books, and one day he got a personally signed autographed picture of you and Trigger for me—one of the happiest moments of my life. I'll always remember how thrilled I was when he gave it to me. I'm professor of clarinet at Michigan State University now but still a fan! This was brought home to me when in Teton Village, Wyoming. I went to a fine restaurant called Mangy Moose where there is a Roy Rogers room with all sorts of posters from your movies, etc. I was thrilled all over again. It must make you feel wonderful to know how much you gave to so many people, and your high moral standards through the years have been a model few stars can match. I just wanted to say how much I admired your movies, your life, your adoptions, and your wife as well. I wish you all the best.

Elsa Ludewig Verderber, East Lansing, MI - 10/14/96

(Ms. Verderber is the clarinetist with the renowned, piano-clarinet-violin chamber group, the Verdehr Trio.)

---

to – Roy

I have loved you since I was a little girl. I have a picture of you and me when you opened a Roy Rogers Restaurant here in Philadelphia. It is one of my very special treasures! I was thrilled beyond belief. I could not believe I was with you and that you put your arm around me. My mother had all of Dale's books, and now I have them. She would read the book, *Angel Unaware*, and cry. She thought it was so beautiful. You will always be King of the Cowboys to us, and you are always in our thoughts and prayers.

Margie and Chuck Cowell, Roslyn, PA – 10/8/96

to – Dale

I just needed to write to let you know how much you, Dale Evans, and your late, great husband meant to me as a child, and, as an adult. All class! What prompted me to write was a truly unique (or weird) experience! As I was cleaning out an old attic, I found my Roy Rogers-Dale Evans lunch box and thermos from the 50s/60s—fond, fond memories of grade school and Saturday mornings with my favorite cowboy. Now the weird part...that very day on AMC (American Movie Channel) was a 1950 movie, "Trigger Jr.," and from start to finish there were tears flowing down my cheeks—tears of joy! Memories of a much simpler time, spending time with my best friends—Roy, Dale, Trigger, Bullet and Buttermilk. Thanks for many wonderful memories!

Bob Mazzolini, Bay Village, OH - 1/25/99

1950s - Bob Mazzolini (in cowboy hat) with best friend (in coon skin cap)

1956 - Bob Mazzolini – ready for the bad guys
- adult and child photos of Bob Mazzolini provided by Mary Jo Mazzolini

to – Dale

THEN (9/11/98): Roy's life, and the image he projected, touched millions of people all over the world. I am merely one of those upon whom Roy had a positive and perhaps critical influence. I never knew my folks and was raised in various "homes" and orphanages. In 1950, I was five years old and residing in an orphanage located in a ranch outside of Sparks, Nevada. I saw my first movie, and it starred Roy Rogers. From that moment on, Roy became my role model. He defined what and who a hero and a man should be. My prize possessions were a two-gun, Roy Rogers cap gun-and-holster set and a stick horse named, of course, Trigger. For reasons unimportant here, my first great sense of loss came when those items, which I slept with (I left Trigger loose because I knew he would never leave me) were taken from me, and I was never allowed to see another movie until I was 15 years old. I was almost six when these events occurred, but I missed Roy terribly. I would stand outside the movie theater in the dusty little towns, gaze at the marquees, and imagine all of the exciting, wonderful, and heroic deeds Roy was accomplishing. I used to wish Roy were my dad. My love of horses was influenced by Roy's obvious rapport with, and kindness to, horses. And, of course, I was fascinated with his guns. Consequently, horses, guns and "doing the right thing" were what Roy represented to me. Over the years, I have been a working cowboy, professional western horse trainer, world class pistol champion, combat-decorated Green Beret in Vietnam, law enforcement officer, drug agent, and now I am a professor of criminal justice here at Fort Hays State University – the home of Wild Bill Hickock, Buffalo Bill Cody and George Armstrong Custer. Without going into detail, Roy's model and influence, in no small measure, kept me on the straight and narrow. Roy represented the values and motivation which kept me out of prison and provided the necessary guidance to succeed in spite of adversity. His image shaped me in my most formative years, and, as the Bible notes, I've not strayed far from those early teachings. When there were some very tough times growing up, and I was faced with moments of choice regarding right and wrong, I would ask myself "What would Roy do?" Somehow, I always knew those times I fell short, and I felt guilty that I had let my hero down. When I succeeded, and often it was neither the easy nor painless path, I felt that Roy would have been proud of me. Children need approval and I pretended that Roy gave me his. I never had the privilege to meet Roy or you, but Roy provided a lamp and a guiding light in some very dark corners of a young boy's world. When this horseman rides that pale horse upon that dark river into the Shadowland, I hope to lean across my saddle, shake his hand, and simply say, "Thanks, Roy".

NOW – (10/5/11): In the intervening years since writing to Dale, I retired from teaching and now raise horses on a remote ranch in New Mexico. The world is in worse condition now than when I penned my letter to Dale in September of 1998. While growing up in the late 1940s and the 1950s, we were a nation of values, hope and moral certitude. We neither apologized for, nor agonized over, having to do tough things to keep the America of Roy Rogers as a beacon of freedom and hope for the entire world. God figured prominently in Roy's life. Often in his movies there were unashamed quotes from, or references to, the Bible, and we were a better nation for it. I believe Roy represents now, more than ever, the necessity of the values of courage, honor and the morality of a God-fearing nation. Roy made America a better place. *James R. Jarrett – NM* (ABD-ph.d, MS)

James R. Jarrett and his horse, Trooper
- photo provided by James R. Jarrett

to – Roy

I am 59 years old and one of your Saturday afternoon fans in the days when your movies were regular entertainment for kids. You and Dale Evans were just great! Why don't they have good movies like yours for the kids of today? They really need them. I have 4 grandkids who haven't seen any really good movies, like yours, in their whole lives, and they are 6 and 9 years old. Thanks for the many years of good entertainment from you and Dale. Your fans still love you and care about you! And Happy Trails to you! Oh, who could forget that song?

Judith Jones, Amarillo, TX – 10/29/96

to – Roy

When I was a kid going to the movies with my parents, you were my favorite cowboy. When my brother and I played cowboys, we were always Roy Rogers and Dale Evans, or sometimes your children, Sandy and Dusty. I have loved horses my whole life and thought that Trigger, Trigger, Jr., and Buttermilk were the most gorgeous horses I had ever seen. To say that you gave us a lot of entertainment and joy when we were children is an understatement. We may not get to see Roy Rogers' movies now, but my kids know who you are. Thank you for my childhood memories!

Jean Maxwell, Dallas, GA - 11/26/90

to – Dale

Upon the death of Roy Rogers, I have given a great deal of thought as to how this incredible American hero molded a generation of young children for the better. I lost my father two years ago to congestive heart failure at the age of 84 and was holding his hand when he passed away. If I may, I'd like to share with you the impact you and your husband had upon the Coulter household in Attica, Michigan. I was one of ten children, and we lived on a farm where we raised cattle and crops. We lived approximately seven miles from town, and didn't have a lot of money or get to visit with other kids during our summer break from school. As I look back on those times, I did not, nor do I now, feel any way deprived because we were poor farmers. I think that is largely due to what Roy Rogers brought to our generation. My sisters, brothers and I would have to invent our entertainment. We did not have a lot of toys. My sister would pretend she was Dale Evans running a restaurant (mother's kitchen.) At lunch and dinnertime, we would go to Dale's Restaurant and pay her for our meals with play money (strips of old magazines cut in the shape of dollar bills.) We also used bags of gold dust, which was sifted sand in cut-up rags. When not in the restaurant, we would ride the range on our stick horses. Mine, of course, was Trigger. My brother would use Dad's old hankies to cover his face and be the robber. When we would visit my grandmother's home, we would go to a small stand of seedling trees on her property and chop down the perfect, straight stick horse. To make it Trigger, I would strip the bark. Then, because our mother didn't want us to bring the sticks home (she was always afraid we'd fall and hurt ourselves on the sticks,) we would tie them to the bumper of our 1951 Chevrolet automobile with binder twine and take them off after Mother went into the house. Years later we still laugh about these instances, and mother also found the humor in our antics. I never wanted to be the "bad guy." Roy was who I looked up to and wanted to emulate. Today, I am the Coordinator of Victim Services for the County of Lapeer, Michigan. I am still fighting the bad guys, and trying to keep our community a safe place to raise families. I feel sorry for the kids of today and the generations to come, for they do not have the hero that so impacted our lives in such a positive manner. I've truly had many "Happy Trails" in my life, and you and Roy helped give that to each of your little buckaroos by teaching us trust, honesty and respect. I am enclosing a poem I wrote shortly after hearing of the death of my hero, Roy Rogers. Thank you for sharing your life, and your husband, with all of us. So long, and may the good Lord take a likin' to ya!

"My Hero" by Cathy Coulter Strong

My hero died today
I lost a special friend
Although we never met
He touched my life again and again

He taught me respect
Honesty and kindness
We were his little buckaroos
I feel such a sense of sadness

Little did he know
What an impact he had on my life
How he influenced this childhood tomboy
As both a mother and a wife

He was the guy in the white hat
Fighting crime and deceit
I took to the legal profession
Helping to keep the justice he would seek

Each night I would go to bed
And dream of riding with Roy
Did he ever really know
How he influenced each girl and boy?

We were the generation
His little cowgirls and boys
And as I look at this world today
We could sure use a few more "Roys"

I'm about to be a grandmother
And you can rest assured
As I rock that tiny child
I'll be singing "Happy Trails"

I'll tell the next generation
All about my cowboy hero
And tell them how we were so blessed
To have such a wonderful role model

Although I never got to tell him
I wish him happy trails
And to say a great big thank you
From all his little buckaroos

I send this little message
To his loving children and wife
And thank you all so very much
For sharing your cowboy's life

Cathy Coulter Strong, Lapeer, MI - 9/16/98

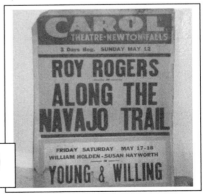

Essay

Ever since I was very young I've been a big Roy Rogers Fan. I never missed his TV Show or his movies when they were on TV on Saturday afternoon. I still have my original Roy Rogers Riders Club Card and the program I got when I was lucky enough to see Roy when I was 8 years old. Dad and Mom knew there was no way I was going let them get by without taking me! That was in 1959 at Roberts Stadium in Evansville, IN. Roy & Dale were traveling the country promoting their TV show. I was in the 7th row, and it was an experience I will never forget.

Today I operate a nonprofit museum in Buckskin, IN. It's called Henager's Memories & Nostalgia, and since the Roy Rogers and Dale Evans Museum closed, we have the largest Roy Rogers exhibit in the country, along with other western stars memorabilia, film and TV treasures, a USO photo library and mementos, and pop culture keepsakes. I had no idea when I was a kid that one day I would grow up to be in charge of an exhibit of my very own western hero, Roy Rogers, the King of the Cowboys. It's an honor."

James Gerald Henager, owner and curator of Henager's Memories and Nostalgia

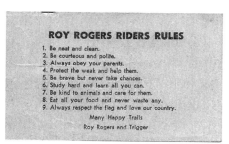

James Gerald Henager's original 1950s Roy Rogers Riders Club card
- card provided by James Henager

Scenes from the Roy Rogers Exhibit
at

Henager's
"Memories and Nostalgia" Museum
Buckskin, IN

- all photos provided by James Henager

Dear Roy Rogers
My name is Jake Howk.
Will you send me an aytograph
picter of you on triger!
I'm you number 1 fan!
How long have you ben in the
Saddle? I'm in seconb grabe.
I'm 7 Years old.
I have a horse named Joy.
My dad used to watch Your TV
shows all the time now
We rent them anb watch ther
on our VCR. I like triger and
the tricks he does. My Birthday is
Febryary 14, I'll pray for you every-
day.
         Your friend Jake Howk

              Bloomfield Iowa
                        52537

Jake Howk, Bloomfield, IA – 11/13/90

to – Roy

I wanted to remind you of a story from years ago when I was teaching Sunday School and the topic was the Crucifixion. One little kid said, "I'll bet they wouldn't have done that if Roy Rogers had been there!" Roy Rogers might be modest, but as years have gone by, I've become convinced the little boy was right! You know, as the gross inadequacies of the entertainment industry becomes more and more commonplace, the high caliber of your commitment in entertainment is even more valued. Blessings to you.

Rev. Phyllis Pottorff-Albrecht, Broomfield, CO - 11/6/90

1948 - A young Phyllis and little sister, Sandra, riding Scout and Flicka
- photo provided by Rev. Phyllis Pottorff-Albrecht

to – Dale

Today I thought of you with good thoughts, and I hope you are doing well. I miss Roy, too. I wanted you to know that you have always been an inspiration to me. I so enjoyed your books, "Angel Unaware" and "Dearest Debbie." And many years ago, after reading your book, "Christmas is Always," I wrote a poem inspired by that book. I'm enclosing a copy, and I hope you enjoy it. Thank you for the memories and the "Happy Trails.

"Christmas is Always" by Barbara Howard

(Inspired by Dale Evans Rogers and her book, *Christmas is Always*)

Have you ever heard the story about the Christmas chime?
It seems it started long ago toward the beginning of time.
To hear the chimes play sweetly, it is said you must give
A gift that comes right from your heart, so that God within it might live.

So along came the rich man with his big bag of gold,
Said, "Here chimes, I have so much I'm afraid that it might mold."
But the chimes remained silent for the man did not give his all.
To have so much and give so little was the rich man's downfall.

Next came the average man who gave what he thought he could afford.
After much pondering and thinking, "It's not enough," sayeth the Lord.
So the chimes remained silent for the man did not give his all.
To have so much and give so little was the average man's downfall.

Finally came a lame boy who had no money at all.
He laid his crutches on the altar and stood there big and tall.
And the chimes began ringing and a peace shown on his face,
As he walked out of that church, God had given his grace.

To give before you can receive is plainly shown here.
The first two were not sincere and did not hold God dear.
So God did not give of his self until he was received.
And it can happen even to you, if you will only believe.

Barbara Howard, Martinsville, IN - 3/11/99

to – Roy

THEN (10/9/96): You don't know what an inspiration you have been to

1968 - Carol Garrett and Roy Rogers
- photo provided by Carol Garrett

me ever since I was a youngster, and even still today. You are needed here to inspire others. God bless you! I had my picture taken with you in Pittsburgh 28 years ago, and I still have it. It was one of the great highlights of my life, and I will treasure it forever.

NOW (7/15/11): I was so excited in the picture that I was crying and biting my lip. I had tears flowing because it was the only time I got close to Roy in my whole life. He was the only hero I ever had in 60 years. I saw almost every picture he made, and I worked when I was a kid just to buy movie magazines with him in it. We cleaned a big church every week so I'd run down to the local magazine place, and if there were no new magazines, I didn't work that week. When I went to see Roy I had an old car, and my son was only 4 years old. I got lost then broke the speed limit to make up time, and still only managed to get one cowboy boot on before I arrived. When we finally arrived, my son had gone to sleep. I poked him and told him, "You aren't going to sleep during the only time in my life to see Roy Rogers!" And he just said, "Who is he, Ma?" Well, we were there, but my camera was out of film. I was so upset. I told a nearby kid that if he'd go across the street and get me some film that I'd give him $5, and he said, *"Lady, I don't want to miss Roy either!"* So I was already dripping tears when this nice lady came up and offered to take my picture with Roy. I promised her a Snoopy dog bank if she'd do that. She did, and I did. We exchanged addresses, and I was so happy when this picture came in the mail. I made the bank and sent it to her. It's an old picture, but hey, we didn't have digital in those days. Here I am, now 73 years old, and I tore the house apart to find this one Roy Rogers picture. I went through closets, cupboards, old mail, new mail, magazines, boxes, a big craft room—three weeks of digging like an archeologist—but I got rid of a lot of stuff that needed booting, and boy did I feel rewarded when I found my poor misplaced picture. The memories are so worth it.

Carol Garrett, Norfolk, VA - 10/8/96

"A Country Happening"
Starring

Roy Rogers and Dale Evans

Bobby Goldsboro
Jody Miller
Glenn Ash
The Ozark Girls
And Special Guest Star
Michael Landon

to – Roy

Being your fan began when I first saw you on the screen. I was a young boy then who became totally taken by a cowboy who portrayed the good part of the West. I never missed a single movie of you and your wonderful horse, Trigger. There wasn't a Saturday afternoon that I didn't go to our local theater to see you in action. Of course, all my friends and I knew it wasn't real, but to us you were real, our hero, a hero that the kids of today could use as an example. The so-called heroes of today portrayed on the screen are poor examples indeed for impressionable young children. You not only carried this persona in the movies but in your daily personal life. With your life companion, Dale, you raised a beautiful family you should be well proud of. Even when tragedy struck your family, you and Dale persevered through it all with your love for each other. As of this writing, I am 66 years old. I have been your fan from your first movie until this moment. I collect all your movies and have shown them to my children and now my grandchildren. I read an article that said you need your fans, but I beg to differ. It is us who need you. Always.

Joseph Matteo, Tacoma, WA - 10/10/96

to – Roy and Dale

I'm so glad to write to both of you to tell you how very much I've enjoyed you over the years. Roy, you will always be the King of the Cowboys to me, and Trigger will always have a place in my heart! As a preteen girl I was very horse crazy. I wanted a horse of my own in the worst way, so much so that I took every opportunity to take riding lessons, go to horse camp, etc. I was so crazy about horses that I even pretended to be one! I ran and acted like a horse, constantly drew horses, and was always reading about them. I took it to such extremes that I made my bicycle into "Trigger," the fastest "horse" on the block. My neighbor let me draw a horse head of Trigger on plywood. He cut it out, put reins of leather and a metal bit on it, and attached it to the handlebars of my bike. "Trigger's tail was made of yarn, and I removed the seat "saddle" every night. I put "him" in a stall I made with straw (weeds,) and made sure there was water to drink! I guess everyone thought I was a real nut, but I didn't care at the time. Then, when I was in the fifth grade, the cutest boy in the class decided he wanted to come by my house and visit. Everything was fine until he saw my bike decked out like a horse. He looked at me like I was crazy and took off pronto! That did it. The horse head had to go because I'd discovered boys! I still chuckle about it. How I would love to meet you and to see your museum. That would be such a thrill! Your influence was always such a positive one in my formative years. I wish my kids had a "hero" like you in this day and age. I am a devoted fan who keeps you both in my prayers.

Carolyn S. Voskamp, San Carlos, CA - 10/13/96

to – Roy

I just want to thank you for all the wonderful memories I have of growing up and having you to love. What a pity that my own children do not have that same type of guide coming from Hollywood today. I wish to thank you for the visual effect of the Double R gates in front of your home and for your museum. The museum is a gift to us, your fans, and I thank you so much for it. About four years ago, my husband gave me my dream of visiting your museum, and we drove by where you live. What a thrill! I just stood outside your gates, and all the years of loving you and respecting you came to mind and washed over me. I still can't believe I've been there until I look at the slides we took. I must say we were very nervous. The golfers watched us to see what we were doing, and believe me, we took our pictures fast! I've had the enclosed program in my scrapbook since my husband took me to the American Royal in 1971. I thought you might want it for your collection. I didn't note one at the museum when we were there. It's sent with all my best wishes.

Joan M. Hummel, Americus, KS - 11/6/90

1971 Royal Livestock and Horse Show Program

- program provided by Joan Hummel

to – Dale

THEN (1/18/99): I hope this letter finds you well. Last July I had the pleasure of meeting you for the first time at the museum. Without a doubt, it was a dream come true for me. Ever since I was a little girl and watched you on TV, I had dreamed of meeting you. DREAMS DO COME TRUE! However, my real reason for writing is to pass along a wonderful story which is guaranteed to put a smile on your face and joy in your heart. Last summer when my mother, aunt, and I were at the museum, my aunt bought some Roy Rogers and Dale Evans t-shirts to take home to her great grandchildren in Texas. Their names are Allie and Murphey. When Murphey, age 5, got his t-shirt, he looked up and said, "Who's Roy Rogers?" Everyone there was, "Why, he's the King of the Cowboys." Then Murphey thought for a bit and said he would like to see a show of Roy Rogers and see what he looks like because someday *he* was going to be the King of the Cowboys! Then his little sister, Allie, piped up and said, "If he's going to be a singing cowboy, what am I going to be?" Everyone laughed and said, "You'll be the Queen of the West!" So needless to say, you two won the hearts of two little children who hadn't yet seen any of your shows or heard your music. But, never fear, that has been resolved! My mother, here in California, just bought four of your TV shows and is sending them to Allie and Murphey. Your legacy continues! You two, who have brought such joy to so many of us while growing up, still impress and influence the next generation! You are loved and we are all blessed to have been a part of the wonderful saga of Roy Rogers and Dale Evans. Thank you for your love and sharing of so much of your lives. We feel like we know you! And in a way I do. A few years back you handwrote me the loveliest note in answer to one of mine when I asked the origin of "The Bible Tells Me So" song. That treasured letter from you is framed and on my wall. May God continue to bless and keep you healthy and happy. Much love to you.

NOW (7/4/11): Roy and Dale were truly one in a million. I loved and respected them so much. I remember meeting Roy in 1995. I had been in the lobby of the museum for a couple of hours before he arrived. The reason that the meeting was so memorable was (a) because I had never seen him in person before, and most importantly (b) I got to see his devotion to children first hand.

A very young child was on what looked like a mobile hospital bed, flat out, but low to the ground. Roy walked through the door and entered the lobby, saw the child and immediately walked over to the bed. With obvious difficulty he got down on his knees, took that child's hand and talked and talked. I don't know what was said, but it was a soothing sound and he kept patting the child's hand he was holding. After about 5 minutes he struggled to get back to his feet, but before he stood up straight, he kissed the child. It brought tears to my eyes. It was especially nice because other people in the lobby, including me, respectfully kept our distance until he was done. I'd heard many times of the things he's done with and for children, but it was the opportunity of a lifetime for me to see him as the man he was. It was after that incredible experience that I had my picture taken with him. Several years later, after Roy had died, my family and I were back in Victorville and went to the museum to show my aunt and uncle who'd never been there. Lo and behold, in comes Dale Evans. I'd never met her, just gotten a handwritten letter acknowledging a letter I'd sent her. And now, in subsequent years, I've been twice to the cemetery to pay my respects. What a peaceful place that is. They were VERY special people. And who would have thought when I, as a child, put on my red cowboy hat and my gun and holster, and went in to watch them on their show, that I would remember it as if it were yesterday instead of over 50 years ago! I, for one, wish there were more people like them in this world.

Nancy Graf, Carmichael, CA

Roy Rogers and Nancy Graf — Nancy Graf and family with Dale Evans
- photos provided by Nancy Graf

Sunday

Dear Nancy,
Thank you for your sweet letter - and for your kind words about "The Bible Tells Me So" - The Lord gave me the words & music in my dressing room when we were filming our T.V. series - It was written in 20 minutes & sung at the end of one of the episodes -
Thank you for the poem - - Lovely -
You could call Cheryl Barnett, our daughter, when you are here & perhaps if we are in town, we could say hello.
God bless you, Nancy!
Dale Evans Rogers

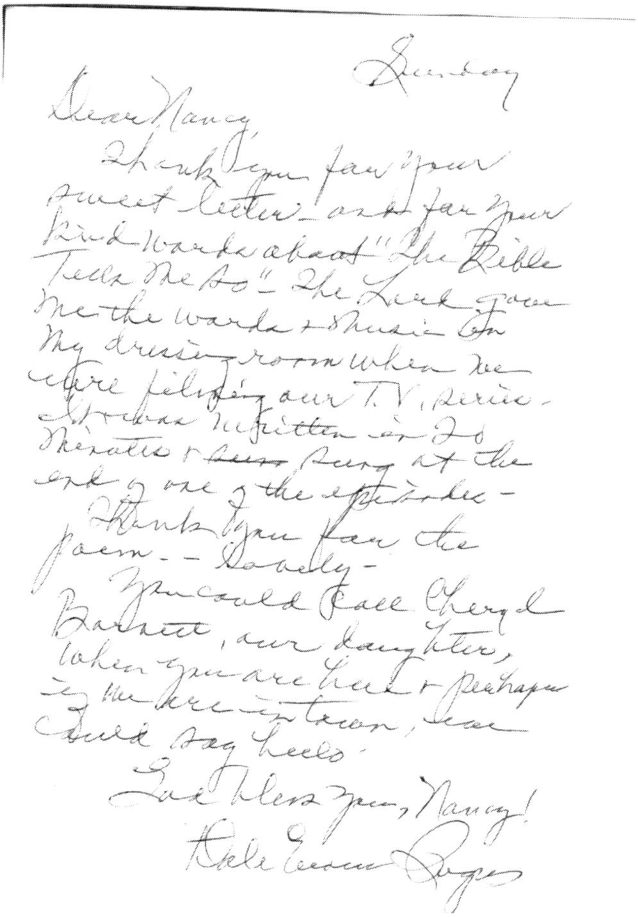

Letter to Nancy Graf from Dale Evans
- letter provided by Nancy Graf

Dear Nancy,

Thank you for your sweet letter and for your kind words about "The Bible Tells Me So." The Lord gave me the words and music in my dressing room when we were filming our T.V. series. It was written in 20 minutes and sung at the end of one of the episodes. Thank you for the poem – lovely. You could call Cheryl Barnett, our daughter, when you are here and perhaps if we are in town, we could say hello." God bless you, Nancy!

Dale Evans Rogers

to – Dale

THEN (1/11/99): The rose on this stationery is for you. You deserve real roses, but this is from my heart. Christmas 1998 must have been hard for you without Roy. At church Sunday morning eight children were dedicated, and during the service our pastor said, "Dale Evans and Roy Rogers have done so much to help awaken the people to the plight of children." You have probably heard this many times over, but I'd like to add my thanks, too. And I just wanted you to have the rose and to feel my respect and admiration.

NOW (7/20/11): In Los Angeles 1986, at a social gathering preceding the Golden Boot Awards, I went up the elevator into a hallway separating two large rooms. I went into the room on the right and visited with several film personalities. Wandering around, and from the hallway, I glanced into the other room. There was Roy Rogers, Dale Evans, and actors Bob Steele and Victor French. Bob was already seated, and I was close enough to see Roy sit down on Bob's knee. Roy laughingly said, "Bob, you are my favorite actor. I've been watching your movies since I was a little boy." (There are only four years age difference between them.) Bob replied, "Why, you are full of it, aren't you? You're as old as I am!" I asked to snap a picture. They both nodded and kept on joking with each other. Dale was standing nearby, shaking her head from side to side. She turned to me, asking, "What am I going to do with them?" Dale asked that I send them a copy of that picture. I did so, along with another that I was included in. They were kind enough to sign the one I was in and return it to me. It was signed in gold colored ink, a nice reminder that the occasion was the Golden Boot Awards. Actor, Victor French is also in the photos. Such wonderful memories I have of the King of the Cowboys and the Queen of the West.

Marietta Thompson, Tuckerman, AR

60

Dale Evans, Roy Rogers, Victor French, Bob Steele
- photo provided by Marietta Thompson

Roy Rogers, Marietta Thompson, Dale Evans, Victor French
- photo provided by Marietta Thompson

to - Dale

You and Roy were my childhood heroes. I am almost 65 years old and grew up near the small Kansas town of Greeley. I was raised by my grandparents on a farm. Every Monday night a tent show came to town. I would sit on the front porch facing the road and watch the people go by as they were going to the show. Grandad drove an old "Star" car, and the only time we went to town was on Saturday to grocery shop. His eyesight was going bad. Well, I was given a choice of a special movie I could go to once in awhile. So I waited for a Roy Rogers and Dale Evans movie to come to town. Then, bless their hearts, they would take me to town to see the show, and wait in the car till the show was over (Grandma was crippled.) I will never forget that! I waited for shows that you and Roy were both in. Since then I have been able to buy movies on tape, since I missed so many when they first came out. I always felt like you two were someone I would like to know, and I always thought you were so pretty, and you still are. It was my lifelong dream to meet you and Roy in person, but never made it. I was devastated when I heard the news of Roy's passing over the car radio at 6:30 am. I was coming home from work. I couldn't sleep that day. I just cried all day. Now I watch you every Saturday on "A Date With Dale." This is Saturday, and your show is coming on. Your hair is fixed so beautiful, red hair band, beautiful black and red dress, and the love of Jesus radiates from your face. I am hearing you now. I loved that song you just sang. And I am looking forward to your new book. If it is the Lord's will, maybe after I retire, I will be able to meet you one day. I would so much love to. You are such a blessing to us all.

Betty Chadwell, Mauriceville, TX - 9/12/98

61

to – Dale

As I watched your segment of TBN Today I was so moved—once again. Your *Angel Unaware* story made me cry with deep emotion and brought to mind much suffering I had experienced as a child when I had been severely water-burned over the entire front of my body. This was around 1955. My mother nursed me according to the doctor's instructions. I slept on sterile sheets that my mother had to put in the oven first. She had to use sterile water to soak gauze to place on my eyes and lips so they wouldn't heal closed and had to tent the cover sheet so it wouldn't touch my body. The only thing I could do for months was lay there and watch the shows on TV that she approved of. I can joyfully say that watching Roy Rogers and Dale Evans was one of those cherished programs. You taught wonderful principles that helped me throughout my life. I wanted everything with you or your husband on it, especially the lunch box. But we were too poor to afford "luxuries." I should have written to you some 40 years ago just to share my love for you both. Through the years I always looked forward to any special Roy would have on TV—Roy appearing with the performing stallions, especially. During the months I spent in bed as a child you and Roy were my very own "angels unaware." Even now, words can never say how much I love you and your husband and the strength of character and Christian example you have both boldly lived. You have touched so many lives. Thank you.

Debbie Waddell, Colorado Springs, CO - 2/20/99

Dale Evans on Trigger
with Roy Rogers
- photo provided by the Rogers
Family

to – Roy and Dale

THEN (12/15/90): We think of the two of you so very often, and hope you are both doing fine. Hopefully our "trails" will meet again soon. We wish you and your family peace and health and happiness.

NOW: (8/1/11): We had the pleasure of meeting Roy and Dale several times in the mid-to-late 1980s. Mondo even spent a few days with them at their museum and their home. Talk about walking on air for months! Just looking at the photo of Mondo with Roy and Dale, anyone can see how truly sincere and happy Roy and Dale were to pose for the picture. And that was the way for everyone they met! They were two very extraordinary people.

Mondo and Mary Lou Polverari, Wallingford, CT

Roy Rogers, Dale Evans and Mondo Polverari
- photo provided by Mary Lou and Mondo Polverari

Original art of Roy, Dale and Trigger created by Armand "Mondo" Polverari
and approved by Roy Rogers and Dale Evans in the 1980s
- art provided by Mondo and Mary Lou Polverari

---

to – Roy

You have always been my hero. The lessons you taught me about good vs. bad must have done a lot of good. I am a police officer now.

Detective H., (state withheld)

---

to – Dale

I realize that it has been several months since the passing of your husband, Roy. Thinking that it might comfort you to understand that Roy's fans still think of him, and you, after all the media coverage is over, I thought I would write and in my most inadequate way express my personal sorrow to you and to say how much I miss him, too. While I am 48 years old, I cried for almost an hour upon learning of his passing. You see, when I was a child and anyone ever asked me what I wanted to be when I grew up, I always responded "Roy Rogers!" It never entered my mind to want to be anything else. But unfortunately that position was already taken, so I settled for a job as a postal manager. I feel so sorry for today's children with the idols and icons they label as their heroes. Roy never made a three-point shot in basketball, hit a home run in baseball, or ran the one-hundred-yard dash in 10 seconds flat. All he did was set a perfect example for the children of the world and be someone we all could look up to and admire and want to be like. I never wanted to "be like Mike." I wanted to be like Roy. I recall as vividly as if it were yesterday how my older brother and I would dress up like Roy Rogers and would chase all the "bad" people from our neighborhood. Guns blazing as we rode our wooden horse our father had made for us, I am sure we were a sight to behold. The only problem was deciding who got to be Roy. There were no more vicious battles in the history of playing cowboys than those that decided who got to be Roy and who got to be Pat Brady. I got the spanking of my life when I (and my faithful metal vacuum hose) convinced my brother that I was going to be Roy that afternoon. I acted very un-Roy-like by whopping my brother several times until he conceded and I got to be Roy. When my brother was not home I got to be Roy and my grandmother was you. I have enclosed a photo of my brother and I dressing up to play "Roy Rogers." I am the good-looking one on the right holding a cool glass of water. Playing "Roy" was a tough job, and I needed refreshment. Each night I was sung to sleep by the "King of the Cowboys" as the record player scratched out "Happy Trails." The world will never see the likes of Roy Rogers again, and I feel sorry for our children that they never got to know him like my age group did. He was such a special human being, always on the side of what was good, and staunchly opposed to what was bad or evil.

Who can today's children identify with that will support such ideals? I don't know of anyone. Such a pity. So "Happy Trails" to you, Ms. Evans, and when you see Roy again, tell him that we still miss him and love him just as we still love you.

Mike Slentz, Greenville, NC - 9/30/98

1953 – Mike Slentz (drinking) and brother, Harvey,
hitting the chuck wagon between bad guy chases
- photo provided by Mike Slentz

---

to – Roy

I was born in Guatemala, Central America. You made us so very happy there—you and Trigger and your dog, Bullet. I hope you know that people from foreign countries love you, too. We remember.

R.M., Guatemala, Central America

Not too many people reading this who were alive in 1950 can tell you where they were or what they were doing on the afternoon of December 3, 1950. I can! That is the day the Roy Rogers Show, "Live and in Person" came to the stage of the War Memorial Auditorium in my hometown, Birmingham, AL. I was only eight years old at the time, but I remember it clearly.

My family and I arrived early, and the first thing we saw was Roy's truck and trailer parked by the curb in front of the auditorium. On the side of the big trailer was a larger-than-life color picture of Roy on a rearing Trigger. Through the open side door of the trailer, I could see Trigger inside. A man was brushing him, getting him ready for the show. At the time, I thought to myself, when I grow up, I want to take care of Trigger and drive Roy's truck and trailer. That was my life ambition for a while, when I was a kid.

I remember the auditorium was packed to capacity that day. The Sons of the Pioneers sang lots of great songs with Roy and Dale and I remember Roy shooting aerial targets (inside the building) tossed up by Pat Brady. Even then, I wondered how Roy could shoot up at the ceiling without putting a hole through the roof. Sixty years later, I learned he was shooting special shot shells out of his six-guns, designed to break glass balls without doing any other damage. I also remember the great costumes Roy and Dale wore, but most of all, I remember Roy and Trigger. I became a big fan of Roy's that day, and have remained one all my life.

As I walked up Waalew Road in Apple Valley, CA on that hot July afternoon in 1998, to the entrance of Sunset Hills Memorial Park, one of the eight Single Action Shooting Society Honor Guards preceding Roy's horse drawn hearse, I thought about that December day in Alabama. I thought about the paths of life and the choices that led me across the country and across the years to that final moment with Roy, in the setting sun of the California desert. I thought about the influence Roy had on my life and the lives of most of us who

265

try to follow *The Cowboy Way*. I reflected on the privilege I had of knowing Roy Rogers and how proud I felt to be one of his Honor Guards. Truly it was another day with the King of the Cowboys that I will never forget.

Joel "Dutch" Dortch, Executive Director of the Happy Trails Children's Foundation, in Apple Valley, CA and 1998-2007 producer of the annual Roy Rogers and Dale Evans Western Film Festival, in the Victorville/Apple Valley area, a fundraiser for the Happy Trails Children's Foundation.

Roy Rogers and Dale Evans played a major role in helping to establish the Happy Trails Children's Foundation. The foundation built the Cooper Home in Apple Valley, CA to provide a safe haven for children in crisis, who have been severely abused, abandoned or neglected. The foundation is proud to carry on the important work with abused children who were so important to Roy and Dale.

Roy Rogers and Joel "Dutch" Dortch
- photo provided by Joel Dortch

The Happy Trails Children's Foundation is a non-profit, tax-exempt charitable organization

"Papa"

"King of the Cowboys"
"One of the good guys"
"The hero with a white hat that always catches the outlaw"
"He always stands for justice and honor and everything that is right and truthful"

All of these words are reminders of a man named "Roy Rogers" who captured the hearts of young people all over the world and gave them inspiration and hope in this life. He taught them to be honest and to have a love for God and their country. He taught them the importance of family life, going to church, and reading the Bible. He was a "one-of-a-kind" person, and there will never be another like him. HE WAS AN AWESOME HERO.

I also want to share with you a man named Leonard Franklin Slye, a country boy who loved hunting and fishing, and his favorite "coon dog" named Blue. Leonard was shy and hard-working, and God blessed him with a wonderful voice and the talent of a musical family. Leonard was mischievous and fun loving and one who hated to lose at any competition. He went to work at an early age to help support his family. He worked in a shoe factory, drove a truck, and picked fruit to make ends meet. Sometimes he even went "frog gigging" on the canal banks for something to eat. He loved his parents and family, and when God blessed him with success in his life, he never forgot his roots, and he willingly shared his blessings with others. HE WAS A WONDERFUL MAN.

Finally, I want to share with you a man simply called "Dad" or "Papa." He loved his family and provided for their needs while teaching his children the value of a dollar and the importance of working hard and never expecting to get something for nothing. As children, we shared our "Papa" with kids in every country around the world. He could walk into a hospital ward, and the faces of those kids would light up with a new hope and a will to get well. We shared our "Papa" with studios, movie theaters, state fairs, rodeos, recording sessions, radio programs, location sites, and all kinds of public appearances. His fans adored him, and the lessons he taught in all of these places were the same lessons he taught us at home—lessons on honesty, truthfulness, being fair, equality for everyone, responsibility, and never making fun of those who were different. HE WAS A VERY SPECIAL FATHER.

We share our "Papa" with the world all of our lives, and in death, we are sharing him again. But we cannot forget that God shared him first with us. He loaned us this AWESOME HERO, WONDERFUL MAN, and VERY SPECIAL FATHER for 86 years, and we are truly grateful for the time we've had. The world will be a different place without him, but he has left footprints on the sands of time that can never be erased.

I love you, Papa, and I'll see you in the morning.

Your daughter, Linda"

"Mama Dale"

That's the name we gave her when she joined our family on New Year's Eve in 1947. My sister, Cheryl, was 7. I was 4, and my brother, Dusty, was a year old. I'm sure we were a handful for "Mama Dale," but she had the patience to deal with our mistrust, doubt and resentment. Our mother, Arline, had passed away one year earlier, and in our minds we weren't ready yet for anyone to take her place. Mama Dale had her work cut out for her.

Shortly after she joined our earthly family, she joined an even more important family, the family of God. This decision would change her life forever and give her the tools she needed to begin building a spiritual family. We began going to Sunday School and Church and learning about Jesus, the One who would truly make us a family.

Through the years, and the "ups" and "downs" of life, we watched her sustaining faith strengthen her through the loss of 3 children, her parents and brother, and her husband of 50 years. She successfully managed a home and career at the same time and trusted in the Lord to use her for His glory. Once she committed her life to the Lord there was no turning back. She made a vow to witness for Him all her life, and she has completed that vow. I believe she could say these words with the Apostle Paul in II Tim. 4:7: *"I HAVE FOUGHT THE GOOD FIGHT. I HAVE FINISHED THE RACE. I HAVE KEPT THE FAITH."*

Mom has been an inspiration to thousands of people who have read her books through the years. She has touched hearts and lives for the Lord in ways that no other could. She has been God's faithful servant, and she is now reaping the benefits of her faithfulness. She has stepped hand in hand into eternity with Jesus, and she has heard those precious words of His in Matt. 24:23: *"WELL DONE, THOU GOOD AND FAITHFUL SERVENT...ENTER THOU INTO THE JOY OF THE LORD."*

We praise God for the 88 years He loaned Mom to us, and for her faithfulness in pointing us to Jesus that we might receive His gift of salvation. She stood strong for the Lord in our family, and she was obedient to the words of Jesus in Rev. 2:10: *"BE THOU FAITHFUL UNTO DEATH, AND I WILL GIVE YOU A CROWN OF LIFE."* She has received her crown and her gift of eternal life, and is rejoicing in the presence of her Lord and Savior, Jesus Christ.

We're all going to miss her faith, her strength, and her spiritual wisdom, but we'll be looking forward to seeing her again in glory. Thank you, Jesus, for giving our family an amazing "MOM" and thank you, Jesus, for your Amazing Grace.

I love you, Mom, and I'll see you in the morning.

Your daughter, Linda.

Linda Lou (Rogers) Johnson

Messages in stone stand vigil at Roy and Dale's final resting place at Sunset Hills Memorial Park

Roy Rogers and Dale Evans
The King of the Cowboys and the Queen of the West
- photo provided by the Rogers Family

They touched lives, and their legacy lives. They are much loved.

THE TOUCH OF ROY AND DALE
VOLUME II

2011 celebrated what would have been Roy's 100th birthday, and 2012 is that time for Dale. There are many more Roy and Dale stories to tell, and *The Touch of Roy and Dale, Volume II* is already on the horizon. Like this edition, it promises to be filled to the brim with heart and soul.

Further attempts are being made to reach the writers, (or their heirs,) of many wonderful letters that didn't make it into this book. More inspiring essays along with some incredible and candid Roy, Dale and Trigger photos, poetry, art, songs and memorabilia are yet to be shared.

If Roy and Dale influenced your life and you wish to add your voice to the second half of this dual tribute to the King of the Cowboys and the Queen of the West, send your materials to:

The Touch of Roy and Dale
PO Box 70669
Riverside, CA 92513

Happy Trails!

Roy and Dale at home
- photo provided by the Rogers Family

HORSESHOE PHOTOS:

The horseshoe-designated photos in this book represent a selection of the items owned by Roy Rogers and Dale Evans and purchased at the Rogers' home and museum estate sales.

 Original painting by Loviathan Skelton (wife of Red Skelton)

 Carved wood Roy & Dale signs

 Handcrafted chuck wagon diorama

 Palomino horse figure with chain reins

 Roy Rogers Roast Beef ad – Roy Rogers Restaurants

 Miniature cast iron stove with accessories

 Roy Rogers Signature Edition Mossberg Rifle Box

 Horse halter from the Rogers stables

 Roy Rogers Kilgore "Shootin' Iron" gun

10

1943 Magazine ad - Republic Pictures Roy Rogers movie "Idaho"

11

Roy Rogers and Trigger glass and wood mug

12

Dale Evans' Nathan Turk rhinestone steer head outfit

13

Cast iron Coca Cola® wagon

14

1950s Roy Rogers Souvenir Program

15

1965 Hollywood Palace poster

16

1950s Happy Trails Roy Rogers Pennant

17

Happy Trails t-shirt

18

1950 *The Standard Book of Hunting and Shooting*
by Robert B. Stringfellow – gift to Roy

19

Wood and leather bellows

20

Frosted angel figurine

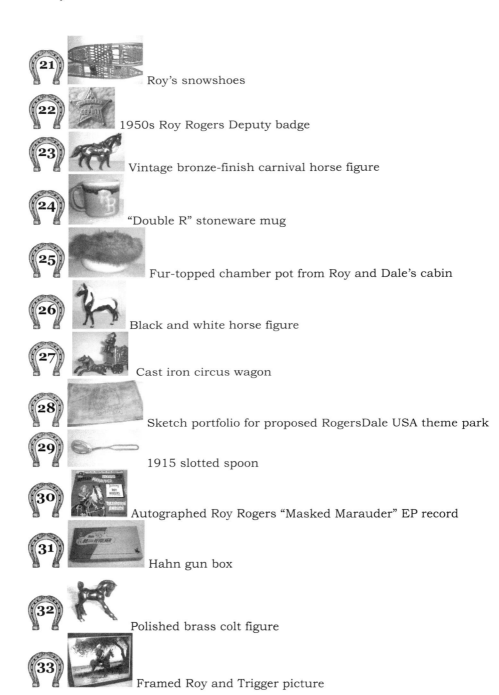

21. Roy's snowshoes

22. 1950s Roy Rogers Deputy badge

23. Vintage bronze-finish carnival horse figure

24. "Double R" stoneware mug

25. Fur-topped chamber pot from Roy and Dale's cabin

26. Black and white horse figure

27. Cast iron circus wagon

28. Sketch portfolio for proposed RogersDale USA theme park

29. 1915 slotted spoon

30. Autographed Roy Rogers "Masked Marauder" EP record

31. Hahn gun box

32. Polished brass colt figure

33. Framed Roy and Trigger picture

34 Antique horse bridle with cricket bit

35 Vintage metal horse clock

36 1950s McCoy Indian Head cookie jar

37 1800s Indian doll made by Iron Eyes Cody's grandmother

38 Antique Indian tobacco cutting board

39 Vintage horsehair saddle girth

40 Dale Evans silk jacket

41 Polished brass resting colt figure

42 Roy Rogers Festival Flag

43 Steer horns signed by Roy "Dusty" Rogers, Jr.

44 Funny horse head bottle opener

45 Original 1930s *Shine On Harvest Moon* movie poster

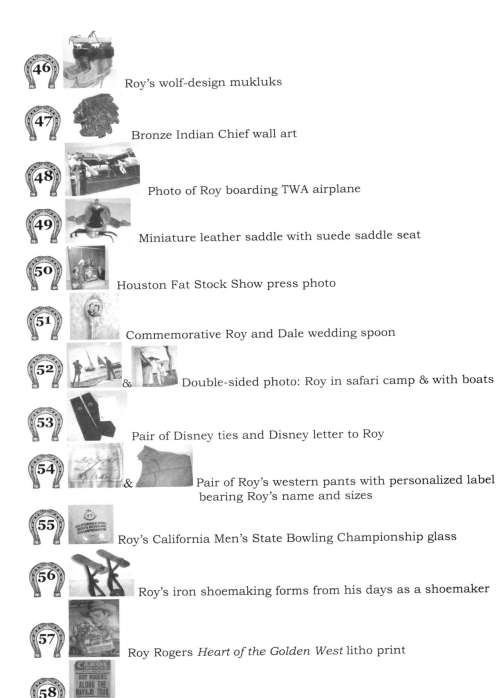

46   Roy's wolf-design mukluks

47   Bronze Indian Chief wall art

48   Photo of Roy boarding TWA airplane

49   Miniature leather saddle with suede saddle seat

50   Houston Fat Stock Show press photo

51   Commemorative Roy and Dale wedding spoon

52   & Double-sided photo: Roy in safari camp & with boats

53   Pair of Disney ties and Disney letter to Roy

54   & Pair of Roy's western pants with personalized label bearing Roy's name and sizes

55   Roy's California Men's State Bowling Championship glass

56   Roy's iron shoemaking forms from his days as a shoemaker

57   Roy Rogers *Heart of the Golden West* litho print

58   Original Carol Theater *Along the Navajo Trail* poster

59 Roy and Dale's script books from *A Country Happening* TV special

60 1986 Golden Boot Awards coffee mug

61 Dale's leather gloves with adorned cuffs

A note about the photographs in this book:

Some photos on these pages appear grainy or blurry. These old photos, including the ones depicting items from the estate sales, were taken with low-resolution cameras many years ago. Other photos were transferred to *The Touch of Roy and Dale* via less than ideal circumstances, and some were even photocopies. This created a dilemma. Should I include or disregard the less-than-stellar pictures? In a few instances it was possible to revisit the source for a better photo. But in most cases, access to the original subject matter no longer exists, and a "do-over" was not an option.

I ultimately decided that even in their unfortunate state, all the photographs had value. Without them, many enjoyable depictions would go unseen, and *The Touch of Roy and Dale* just wouldn't be the same.

Roy and Dale practiced acceptance, embracing flaws as a natural part of life, and I hope both would have enjoyed each and every photo in this tribute, even the ones that are a long way from being pristine photographic specimens. I hope you enjoyed them, too.

Tricia

CONTRIBUTOR'S INDEX

Page numbers indicate the page where an excerpt or essay begins.